project leader

What the best project leaders know, do and say to get results, every time

Mike Clayton

PEARSON

Harlow, England • London • N······pre • Hong Kong
Tokyo • Seoul • Taipei • New ······ch • Paris • Milan

Pearson Education Limited
Edinburgh Gate
Harlow CM20 2JE
Tel: +44 (0)1279 623623
Fax: +44 (0)1279 431059
Website: www.pearson.com/uk

First published in Great Britain in 2012

ISBN: 978–0–273–75936–2

British Library Cataloguing-in-Publication Data
A catalogue record for this book is available from the British Library

Library of Congress Cataloging-in-Publication Data
Clayton, Mike.
    Brilliant project leader : what the best project leaders know, do and say to
get results, every time / Mike Clayton. -- 1st ed.
        p. cm.
    Includes index.
    ISBN 978-0-273-75936-2 (pbk.)
    1. Project management. 2. Leadership. I. Title.
    HD69.P75.C52228 2012
    658.4'092--dc23
                            2011038649

10 9 8 7 6 5 4 3 2 1
15 14 13 12 11

Typeset in 10pt Plantin by 3
Printed and bound in Great Britain by Henry Ling Ltd, Dorchester, Dorset

This book is dedicated to all of the friends, colleagues and clients who helped me to learn the craft of project leadership and who gave me opportunities to practise describing it.

Contents

About the author

Project management: art or science?

Neither, says Mike Clayton. Rather, Mike sees good project management as a craft: precision and elegance combined to produce something that is beautiful, has a form that fits its purpose perfectly, and is eminently useful.

Like art, science and craft, project management is a human activity. As a project manager, Mike firmly believes that this dimension is under-represented in training, seminars, books and articles. And it is this dimension that defines a project leader.

A lifelong passion: for getting things done

Mike has always been a doer and getter-done. His relentless restlessness to achieve more led him to abandon a promising academic career in physics for the high-pressure enticements of management consultancy, working first with niche public sector consultants CSL Group and then with Deloitte.

Mike first learned project management as many of us do: by doing it and applying his common sense. But with opportunities to manage and lead larger projects, and attend training courses and conferences, he started to hone his technique. An omnivorous reader, Mike seeks out and integrates new ideas from anywhere. He learned from the best of the people he worked with – and from the worst. He started to think of himself as a project leader as well as a project manager.

A second passion: for communicating

Mike's second career – in speaking, facilitating and training – allows him to focus on another passion; for communicating ideas and simplifying the complex into easy-to-apply models and techniques. His focus in all of this is on helping people to take what they already know and to extend it so they can be more effective and better respected.

Brilliant Project Leader is Mike's seventh book.

Author acknowledgements

This book would not have been possible without the people who helped me to learn the craft of project leadership, whose advice and example helped me to understand more deeply, and whose presence gave me some helpful anecdotes to tell. There are so many of these people. The following are those who have particularly influenced one or more parts of this book: Colin Bartle-Tubbs, Julian Badcock, Jens Butler, Steve Clark, Guy Dent, Richard England, John Everett, Brian Green, Mark Holmes, Rex Mackrill, Alessandra McConville, George Owen, John Perry, Richard Porter, Tony Quigley, Martyn Watts, Judith Wilks and Nick Wilson.

In my second career, as a speaker, facilitator and trainer, many people and organisations have given me opportunities to road test the ideas in this book and how to present them. In particular: Nick Alcock, Cryss Mennaceur, Oliver Moorby, Phil Sabin, Andrew Tanswell, Perry Timms and, especially, Ron Rosenhead.

Most of my opportunities to lead projects were afforded by two organisations. One was Deloitte, with whom I was a consultant and later senior manager, over a period of 12 years, and for whom I led great teams of talented people for world-class clients. Within Deloitte, I was part of a fantastic team called Programme Leadership, inspirationally led by Gilbert Toppin. The other was Campus Children's Holidays, for whom I volunteered and ran holiday projects for many Liverpool children in the early 1990s.

Finally, I must mention some of the project management bloggers who provide me with the intellectual challenge I miss through no longer being part of an organisation and the great team that I had at Deloitte: Kailash Awati, John Carroll, John Goodpasture, Josh Nankivel and Dan Ward. However, most important of all is to acknowledge that Glen Alleman's kind comments about my blog, *Shift Happens!*, came at just the right time to support my pitch to Pearson Education for this book – thank you, Glen.

Introduction

There is already a very successful book called *Brilliant Project Manager*, so you may be wondering: 'Why *Brilliant Project Leader?*'

To answer this question, we need to define our terms. How does project leadership differ from project management? And what does 'brilliant' mean in this context? Let's take these words one at a time.

Brilliant

A 'brilliant' project is one that potential team members want to join and current team members enjoy being a part of. It is a project that does something new, exciting, important – even wonderful. And, because it is led well, people learn lots, have fun, and create great things that make a real difference.

brilliant exercise

You have been offered a choice of two very different projects to work on. What criteria will you use to decide which project to choose?

Mark was offered a range of projects. Before making a decision, he went to see the project managers of each one. When he made his choice, he elected on the basis of three criteria:

1   *The profile of each project*
Some people will want a high-profile project on which they can make their name and reputation. They fully expect to work very hard, put in long hours and win the chance of advancement. Others prefer a less pressured environment, where they can have more time for their private lives. They accept that the rewards of success may be less evident.

2   *The nature of the project*
What makes Mark say 'brilliant' may be as dull as dust for someone else. But Mark has clear values and also some particular interests. He likes to be stretched intellectually too.

3   *The project manager*
The reason Mark met each project manager was not just to learn about the nature and challenges of each project, but also to get a sense of the person he would be working with. For Mark, a brilliant project begins with a brilliant project leader.

Why 'brilliant' is important

You may have chosen very different criteria, but Mark's represent the three principal reasons why 'brilliant' is important.

1   **Career**
It is no longer the case that careers follow a simple linear pattern. For increasing numbers of us, when we look back from our retirement, we will see that our career is a series of projects.

2   **Projects make change**
When you look back on your career, what difference will you be able to say that you made? Projects change organisations, people, even the world, and success creates something of real value. We need this kind of meaning in our lives to feel fulfilled.

3 6 am

It's 6 am and your alarm goes off: what gets you out of bed and out of the house? It may be selfish, but you need to look forward to going to work or working on your project. No matter how much you need the income, or how important your project is, what motivates many of us equally or more is the fun we have, the things we learn, and the people we work with.

Make every project 'brilliant'

As project leader, every project you lead can be 'brilliant'. And it should be if you are to harness the best work from the best people available to you. More important: I believe that every project *can* be 'brilliant' if you bring passion, commitment and integrity to it.

Project

There are a number of definitions of a project already available, without my adding to the list. Three characteristics recur in most of these definitions:

1 *Temporary*

Projects have a defined start and finish, and are organisational structures that are set up for a single purpose and then dismantled at the end.

2 *Unique*

Most definitions emphasise that projects do something that has not been done before. In the real world, the degree of difference may be small, but when it becomes vanishingly small, we can create greater efficiencies with modern production techniques, and turn our repeated project into 'business as usual'.

3 *Product*

Projects produce something; whether it is an asset, a product, a service, a process, an aim or an outcome.

 brilliant definitions

A project is:

'… a unique, transient endeavour undertaken to achieve a desired outcome'

Association for Project Management (UK based)

'… a temporary endeavour undertaken to create a unique product, service, or result'

Project Management Institute (US based)

Leader

Project management is very much a task-oriented discipline. People are important because they must be allocated to tasks, properly briefed, monitored and supported. Project leadership brings in a far greater focus on your relationships with your team members and the other people linked to your project. It also focuses on your own personal qualities, which determine the extent to which people will willingly follow you: there can be no leadership without followers.

Purple bus leadership

Project leadership goes beyond the project process and is about how you share your vision for what can be. Leaders are able to inspire and motivate others to participate in their project, as well as manage them when they do.

Think about two buses.

The yellow bus

People have to get onto the yellow bus to get where they have to go. It is well-maintained and safely driven. If it breaks down on the way, the driver knows what to do.

The purple bus

People hear the driver of the purple bus talking about the destination, and they want to get on. They enjoy the journey and find it stimulating. They trust the driver and, if the bus breaks down, they all get out and want to help.

Let's look at the two characteristics of leadership that the driver of the purple bus shows.

Leading others

The first cluster of leadership characteristics is what we recognise as 'social skills' – the abilities to understand other people's feelings, concerns, desires and needs, and then use that knowledge effectively, to get the best from those people. As project leader, you need to be able to empathise with the people around you, to sense their mood, read their relationships and master the cultural and political dynamics in and around your project.

You also need to be a consummate communicator, able to forge strong relationships, motivate people to play their part in your project, secure collaboration and cooperation, influence stakeholders at all levels, and handle resistance and conflict. Notice how wide this range of skills is: from building one-to-one rapport with individuals up to inspiring a whole group of people with a compelling vision. Leadership is not easy.

Personal leadership

Yet there is more. Personal leadership refers to the depth of character, the personality traits and the behaviours you exhibit every day – especially when things get tough. These are what attract people to you personally, and build a sense of trust – or not – even before you have an obvious track record. It is more than 'just' charisma or presence, because personal leadership arises from a real depth of character.

The things we associate with great personal leadership are credibility, confidence, self-awareness, consistency, optimism, discipline, resilience, creativity and adaptability, self-control, and, above all, honesty and integrity.

These all start with knowing who you are and what you stand for. A brilliant project leader must know what their values are – in relation to their project and its impact on other areas of their life – and be prepared to defend those values.

'Project leader' versus 'project manager' in a nutshell

If we try to sum up the difference between a project leader and a project manager, we can do so easily, with a table like this.

Project manager	Project leader
Creates a project plan and directs actions	Creates a vision and strategy, and inspires people to act
Project plan for what, how and when to do things	Determines what the organisation needs and why
Focuses on processes, systems and procedures	Focuses on people, their commitment and their ideas
Relies on governance, hierarchies and controls	Inspires transparency, loyalty and trust
Communicates the project plan	Paints a vision of the future
Effective monitor-and-control cycle	Prepared to innovate and make courageous decisions
Works within organisational boundaries	Challenges the boundaries
Does things 'right'	Does the right things
People do what a manager asks because it is their job to	People do what a leader asks because they want to

However, the distinction is not a fair one. No successful manager can ever manage without leading too. And no effective leader can lead a team without being able to manage the people and processes involved.

Moving from management to leadership

When things are straightforward, a project manager needs to do little more than manage, to deliver their project to schedule and on budget. They may want to lead too, to make their project 'brilliant'. But arguably, this is a 'nice to have' addition to their principal role.

However, as times get tougher, people become more uncertain and less confident. Management will not be enough and the tougher things get, the more our project manager must lead their team. Being a project leader has moved from a choice to a necessity.

The structure of *Brilliant Project Leader*

The first two parts of this book look at being a brilliant project leader when it is optional, and you choose to make your project 'brilliant'. The third part is about leading in tough times when leadership is essential, if your project is to succeed.

Part 1: The four essentials of team leadership

There are masses of books written on team leadership, but this part of *Brilliant Project Leader* boils it all down into four essentials.

Chapter 1: You get the team you deserve

Why is leadership important to a project team and why is it so difficult? Why 'you get the team you deserve' and an introduction to the four essentials you *must* focus on, to deserve the team you'd love to have.

Chapter 2: Focus on individuals

The first essential for any team leader is to focus on the personality, needs and capabilities of each individual. This is a vital investment that can harness the diversity of your team to the project's benefit. There may be no 'I' in team, but yes, there is a 'me' and our individuality is the source of the strength of a great team. And don't forget: you too are an individual, so we'll also examine the project leader's own individuality.

Chapter 3: Build and share a clear plan

People feel lost without a sense of direction and if you cannot give one to them, they will lose confidence in you. Work with your team to develop a credible plan and tailor each component of it to the expertise and personal style of each person.

Chapter 4: Foster a true sense of team spirit

What makes a team? Learn the conditions that create a great sense of team spirit and collaboration, and how to put them in place, so that your team feels a shared sense of pride in what they are doing.

Chapter 5: Communicate relentlessly – and well

Good team communication is not negotiable. But what does it mean, and how can you encourage it? How can you articulate your vision for the project in a compelling and persuasive way, and what should you do when conflict arises?

Part 2: Leading your project team at each stage of the project

Part 2 looks at the four stages of a typical project and describes what you can do to lead brilliantly at each stage.

Chapter 6: Project definition stage

As you assemble your team, you must engage and enthuse team members from the beginning. Understand the team's dynamics and transform members into a coherent team that is committed to your project. We also consider the leadership roles in defining your project and setting up a good governance structure, and outline three key skills you will need: managing upwards, stakeholder communication and negotiating.

Chapter 7: Project planning stage

As you get to know your team better, engage them in their own part of your planning activities. Brief them effectively, allocate work, and secure genuine commitment to get the job done – a commitment you will be able to rely upon. You will also learn about the relationship between innovation and risk, and what your options are when your team is distributed over different buildings, cities, countries or even continents.

Chapter 8: Project delivery stage

During delivery of your project, your team will feel under most pressure. Understand how the stresses can affect team dynamics and what you can do to address the problems. What is your team's role in controlling your project and how can you manage their motivation and reward their endeavour?

Chapter 9: Project closure stage

Ironically, after all the effort, many projects remain unfinished simply because the project leader fails to close them down. How can you harness your team to help? What risks do your team pose at this stage, and how can you counter those risks? And what are your final obligations to your team?

Part 3: Project team leadership in tough times

In tough times, leadership takes on a more fundamental role. Part 3 looks at three specific topics.

Chapter 10: Tough times: meeting resistance

Many projects encounter resistance at some stage, and this

can be dispiriting for team members. What is the source of this resistance? How can you and they handle it effectively? And what support can you offer your team?

Chapter 11: Tough times: up against it
What should you do when something goes wrong? For example, sometimes deadlines loom and you need to work faster and harder than you ever planned. What are the secrets to 'crashing your deadlines' and what can you do in the planning stage to foresee and prepare for this scenario?

Chapter 12: Tough times: tough leader
Personal leadership finally comes down to you. We'll examine what you can learn from the fields of positive psychology, influence and stress management to meet the personal challenges of tough times.

'Do I need to know about project management before I read this book?'

The simple answer to this question is 'No, you don't.' This book assumes no basic training in project management, beyond the basic training everyone gets – experiences from life. It is self-contained and my publisher and I have made every effort to ensure that all jargon and technical terms are explained when you first meet them. There is also a handy glossary at the back of the book.

However, this is not a basic book on 'how to manage a project'. Much of what you will need is in here, but for a structured guide to the how of project management, you will need to look elsewhere. The good news is that 80 per cent of project management is organised common sense. If you have that common sense, then you will find much of that organisation in the pages of this book.

PART 1

The four essentials of team leadership

You get the team you deserve. The trick, therefore, is to deserve the team you want. In Part 1, we focus on the four essentials of team leadership:

- The individuals
- The plan
- The team
- Communication

CHAPTER 1

You get the team you deserve

 **brilliant** definition

> A team is a small number of people who collaborate to achieve a shared goal.

We use the term 'team' in a wide variety of contexts from sport to work, so it is hard to encapsulate all of them, and years of research, and metres of shelf space, into a simple definition. This definition has three things: it is short, it is simple and it covers many of the features that research and experience tell us a team should have.

Small number

There is no consensus on how big or small a team can be and still be a team; it is dependent on the situation. However, there is some evidence we can look at. Meredith Belbin's research into teams in the 1970s suggested that ideal workplace teams would have around five members, with a balance of different contributions. Certainly for temporary, largely self-managing teams, five to seven members works well.

At the opposite extreme, it is hard for very large numbers of people to actively collaborate. An example of a large team might be the UK government's Cabinet, which hovers around 20 members (23 at the time of writing, with five non-Cabinet members attending meetings). The extent of active collaboration varies, of course. Once your team grows beyond around 10 or 12 members, coherence and effective intra-team communication become hard to sustain.

In the more popular sports, teams range in size from four (curling) to 18 (Australian rules football). The basic unit of modern Western armies is the squad or section of soldiers, ranging from eight to 12 members, although some forces also use fireteams of four or five men. These latter teams are highly collaborative, based on each person having a clear role, and a simple collective short-term goal. Fireteams work well with experienced and highly trained soldiers, but are not used with inexperienced conscripted soldiers, where a clearer command-and-control structure works better.

It seems that if you have too few members in your team you will lack the breadth of perspectives, specialisms and contributions. There is also the problem that, in a very small team, people can feel isolated and start to want to perform for themselves, rather than the team, possibly leading to competitive behaviours. As the numbers increase too much, the task of coordinating efforts becomes more difficult, and we see the larger team sizes in contexts of greater authoritarian leadership.

So the conclusions are subtle and it must therefore be up to you to decide on the team size that will work best in your situation, and how to divide up a bigger team to get the small-team coherence that you want.

Collaborate

In a good team, members bring complementary skills and approaches. Collaboration brings these together constructively.

One role of a team leader is to find the right balance of harmony and conflict. Too much harmony can lead to stagnation and a little conflict in the mix brings innovation and pressure to succeed. Yet too much conflict will wholly frustrate collaboration and the team will become dysfunctional.

At the core of 'collaboration' is a shared sense of responsibility for producing the results that the team has been charged with. Each member must feel committed to working together and sharing in the trials and

> 'collaboration' is a shared sense of responsibility for producing the results

rewards of the process, with a 'Succeed together, fail together' attitude. Writers and consultants Jon Katzenbach and Douglas Smith suggest that team members should hold themselves 'mutually accountable' for their performance.

Shared goal

Team members need to share an explicit understanding of their purpose. If they are to share responsibility and hold each other accountable, then any differences in understanding the goal will lead to frustration and recriminations. Whilst the written word can still be misunderstood, there is less scope than with spoken words, which can also be mis-recalled. So teams should articulate a written goal, and express it as clearly as possible.

Brilliant project

One valuable asset in creating a brilliant project is a team that will do justice to it by getting the work done efficiently, innovatively and with a sense of passion, commitment and fun. And the truth is that people like being part of a good team.

For many of us, some of our best experiences in work and social lives have been working with a like-minded team of committed friends or colleagues to achieve something challenging and worthwhile.

> ## Mike's first rule of teams
>
> You get the team you deserve.

You get the team you deserve

This rule does not mean that if you are a 'good person' you will get a great team and that if you are, in some way, a 'bad person', the universe will punish you with a bad team. If only life were that fair!

Few of us have the opportunity to hand-pick the 'perfect' team that we want for a job, outside the realm of fantasy football. What Mike's first rule means is that if you take the view that you have the best team you could possibly have, given all the circumstances, and you decide to commit to those people and invest all of your energy in supporting and developing them, then they will work hard to repay you.

If, on the other hand, you think to yourself: 'Well, this is a pretty poor bunch; if only I'd got the other lot' and look for opportunities to prove that they are rubbish, then you will create a self-fulfilling prophecy. To a very real extent, we create our own reality by our thoughts and actions.

So, you get the team you deserve, because the choices you make and the actions you take will determine the extent to which your team will start to shine or finish up rusting.

Getting the team you want

If, however, you could pick your perfect team, how would you do it? What would be your selection criteria? I suggest three:

Diversity

Diversity is not just a handy label or a political imperative: it is one of the most powerful assets a team can have. The more diverse your team is in its skills, experiences, perspectives, approaches, personalities and styles, the more likely it is to succeed.

> The more diverse your team is, the more likely it is to succeed

There is one condition, however, that you must attend to. With diversity comes the potential for conflict – if I see the world differently from you, then we are likely to disagree from time to time. And if we are both passionate about achieving our shared goal, then we are likely to defend our interpretations or ideas equally passionately. As a team leader, you must create an environment where such exchanges are allowed, but are conducted with real respect for each team member's individuality.

Hunger

Favour people who want to be part of your team over those who don't have that hunger to contribute to what you are doing. Recruit people who have a hunger to learn and develop over those who think they already know everything – even if you suspect they are right.

Attitude

You will know what attitudes suit the culture within which your project operates, and the team environment you want to cultivate. Here are four that win with me every time.

1 **Curiosity**
    In the introduction, you saw that projects are, by definition, unique, novel and opportunities to innovate. Curious, creative people who are eager to learn and try out new ideas will be a huge asset.

    There is a common belief that there are, fundamentally, only two things that motivate us as humans: pain and pleasure. This is not true. Humans have a third motivator: curiosity. This desire to answer questions and grow is every bit as powerful and, when your project can harness it, it unleashes a huge potential.

2 Optimism

The novelty of a project also makes it an uncertain venture. I would far rather an optimistic colleague, who is looking for opportunities to succeed, than a pessimist seeking evidence that inevitable failure is around the corner.

3 Cheerfulness

Let's face it: things go wrong, shift happens. Optimism may not be enough, so make sure your team members can see the funny side. I have always felt you don't have to be stern to be serious, so choose a team that will have fun.

4 Conscientiousness

Don't forget that there is a job to do. Hire people who can demonstrate that they will work hard and, because shift happens, will be willing to turn their hands and minds to whatever crops up.

Sadly, you will rarely get the chance to pick the team you want, so you will have to take the best you can get and turn them into the perfect team yourself.

Deserving the team you want

> The team you want is one that will follow you through thick and thin

The team you want is one that will follow you through thick and thin, and think for themselves when you are not there. This will take leadership and a considerable investment of your time and energy.

Leadership

A lot of thinking about leadership has focused on the character-istics, or traits, of leaders, or on the behaviours that will get the best from their team members. These are important subjects that *Brilliant Project Leader* will cover. But, fundamentally, leadership is about the relationship between the leader and their team.

If the relationship is to have any integrity, then it will be based on who the leader really is, and this has come to be termed 'Authentic Leadership'.

> You have to be yourself – the moment you try to be something else, you've had it.

Greg Dyke, former Director-General of the BBC

You can think of 'authenticity' as having four components:

1 A clear sense of purpose, guided by your values

2 Walking the talk, doing what you say and taking responsibility for your decisions

3 Presenting a consistent set of attitudes and behaviours to everyone you meet

4 Being comfortable with who you are and being aware of your strengths and weaknesses.

Sadly, a lot of organisations can undermine authentic leadership by encouraging – or even demanding – conformity. Projects offer a chance to escape this, because each one represents a unique challenge.

The concept of authenticity can track back to the philosopher Heidegger, who makes an important point. To be authentic, we have to respond in our own way to the situation at hand without feeling bound by convention. However, there are limits. Authenticity does not mean we step outside the wider range

being an authentic leader is not a licence to break all rules

of human response – we can only do what 'one does'. So being an authentic leader is not a licence to break all rules – you must conform enough to earn the trust and respect that you need, so you can operate effectively and successfully challenge the norms that need to be questioned.

Investment

In some ways, investing money and resources is the easy part of growing a team. The tough challenge is to find the time to give to your team, so that you can really deserve the best.

A memorable moment in my development as a project leader was a short conversation with a mentor and coach, in which I complained that, no matter how early I got into work, I would soon be interrupted by a team member wanting support, advice or a decision. This was frustrating me, as I was starting to find it hard to do my own portion of work. 'But you are now leading the project, Mike. Supporting your team *is* your job.' That was a real *Aha!* moment for me and from that point on I sought to delegate as much as I could, so that I could spend more time leading my colleagues.

Prioritisation

The key therefore is not to try and add more work into your day, but to prioritise investment in your team above other things and find ways either to say 'no' more often or to get things done in other, less intrusive ways.

brilliant exercise

Make a list of all of your project responsibilities, using three headings:

1 **Leadership**

   Growing, developing, inspiring and supporting your team

2 **Management**

   Planning, controlling and overseeing your project, your people and your resources

3 **Delivery**

   Working on specific activities in your project plan

Now assume that you could get your team into the highest state of performance possible for them by investing fully in leadership. This would still leave your project with the need for management and delivery, of course, but from that assumption, prioritise your list as either:

1 Essential for *me* to do it

2 Ideal for me to do it – but someone else could

3 Better for someone else to do it

4 Not really necessary for anyone to do it.

How does your agenda look now?

Focused investment

If you get a great team, functioning well, you can invest in smoothing rough edges and dealing with difficult issues. Back in the late 1990s, I had such a smooth-running team, and I needed an additional team member with general skills. I'll call the chap who was assigned to my team 'John'.

John came with a health warning. His last two managers had been disappointed with his performance and his days with the firm were numbered. I was asked to make note of any performance issues. I had a different idea, however. In the spirit of 'You get what you look for,' I decided to see if I could find excellence in John's performance. As the rest of the team were performing well and needed less of my time, I invested in supporting John to help him succeed.

The investment started with a frank chat: I had to know whether it was a wise investment. I told John what I'd been told and what I'd decided and I asked him what he wanted: did he want to drift downwards or to prove the other managers wrong? When he confirmed that he wanted to succeed, I knew it was time to invest. To cut a six-month story short; John was a star, who not only did a good job for me, but got a letter of thanks from our client.

Getting the team you deserve

Your earliest days with a new team will set the climate for the team's long-term progress, so here are six steps to get you started.

1. Your very first meetings

Make a real effort to get your first meetings with individual team members and your first team meeting right. Be respectful, thoughtful and passionate about the project. Let people see who you are and let them express who they are. Make time for these meetings and focus more on the style and process than on the content. In Chapter 6, we'll look at the stages of your team's development, so you can be aware of what to expect.

2. Equip your team with the best

Provide the best resources you can to help your team do their work and, throughout the project, fight for ever more and better resources.

3. Be there for them

From day one start a policy of being available to answer questions and provide support. The more you can understand your team's needs, both individually and collectively, the better – and the sooner you start, the stronger your support will be.

4. Listen to your team's ideas

The diversity of your team is the source of its strength, so make time to listen to ideas. They are in the front line, so harness their enthusiasm and creativity.

5. Deal with issues immediately

Sometimes things crop up right from the start and you will be tempted to let them be and hope they will go away. They rarely will. The sources of team failure often have clear early-warning signs and it is far easier to put out a small fire than a raging blaze.

6. Celebrate the new team

Get your team together to recognise who is involved and what they have achieved before now, so that everyone gets a sense of the combined experience and capabilities of the team. Celebrate this, celebrate the challenge before you, and ask people to commit to joining each other and you.

The four essentials

The rest of Part 1 is all about the four essential components of leading a project team. An awful lot has been written about leadership, and many of the fine details hold deep insights and great value. But my assertion and my experience is this:

If you do the basics, and you do them well, and you do them consistently, then you will have a brilliant project team.

Here then are my four essentials:

1   The Individuals

2   The Plan

3   The Team

4   Communication.

It is as simple as that.

But simple is not easy – it takes hard work and commitment to focus on each individual, and the plan, and the team itself, and on excellent communication, continuously, throughout the trials and challenges of delivering a project.

brilliant recap

- A team is a small number of people who collaborate to achieve a shared goal.

- You get the team you deserve.

- The ideal attributes for your team members are diversity, hunger and great attitudes like curiosity, optimism, cheerfulness and conscientiousness.

- Being an authentic leader means being yourself. Commit to this and invest your time and energy in developing your team.

- There are six steps to starting your team off well.

- The four essentials may seem simple, but doing them well is far from easy.

CHAPTER 2

Focus on individuals

There's no "I" in Team' is one of the most commonly quoted pieces of mock wisdom. So it may come as something of a surprise to realise that the character David Brent in the UK TV comedy series *The Office* actually has it right when he says:

'There may be no "I" in team, but there's a "me" if you look hard enough.'

Ricky Gervais and Stephen Merchant

Of course, you know what 'no "I" in team' means. It is about taking the selfish behaviour out of your team contribution, and focusing on the collaboration and shared responsibility. But teams *are* made up of individuals, and if we take our individuality out of the team, then we are left with a bunch of clones. The real strength of your team lies in its diversity: the individual talents, personalities and points of view that each 'me' brings to it.

Team members as individuals

Your job, as project leader, is to get to know each team member as an individual; to find out who they are, what they are good at, what they enjoy and what their hopes and aims are – particularly with respect to your project.

Name

Right from the start, build up your relationship. Get to know each one personally, and begin with the most fundamental thing of all, their name. There is nothing quite as dispiriting as joining a new team and finding that not even the team leader knows your name. Learn the names, and get them right: right pronunciation and right spelling.

People are proud of their names, so asking about spelling and pronunciation are not just practical ways to get them right and help you to remember them; they show that you are taking an interest. If you first hear a name, rather than see it written, ask about its spelling – particularly if it either has more than one common spelling ('Is that Catherine with a C, or Katherine with a K?') or comes from a language you are unfamiliar with. If you first see it written, then ask about pronunciation and don't be afraid to repeat it back and ask if you have it right.

Remembering names is largely a matter of being interested and wanting to remember them. Use the name a couple of times and it will start to stick. Most people who say 'I can't remember names' simply don't take enough trouble to notice the name, or don't care enough to remember it. If you think it is just a small detail that doesn't matter, you are wrong.

 Among the maxims on Lord Naoshige's wall, there was this one: 'Matters of great concern should be treated lightly.' Master Ittei commented, 'Matters of small concern should be treated seriously.'

Yamamoto Tsunetomo, Hagakure

Value

As you learn about each individual, come to value them for who they are and what they can contribute to your project. It is far too easy for us to get into the mode of deprecating people for what they cannot do, and to see only their faults.

You will inevitably find it easier to get to know and to spend time with some members of your team than others. Your role as leader demands that you give equal attention and respect to each person, and avoid overt favouritism or the risk of forming a clique.

> Your role as leader demands that you give equal attention and respect to each person

However, 'equal' attention and respect do not mean 'the same' attention and respect. In the next chapter we will see how it is important to tailor your plan to each individual, to meet their needs and preferences, their style and capabilities. Equal attention and respect mean tailoring your relationship to each person to get the very best from them so that all of your team members have the same chance to perform at their highest level and develop to their full potential.

Respect

Respect is a two-way thing, but it is not symmetrical: you can give it, but you cannot expect it in return. However, you can be sure that if you do not give respect, you won't get real respect back, so start by respecting each team member and, as you get to know them, they will come to know you. Familiarity, your listening and your respect will build liking and respect in the other person, which will pay huge dividends as your project progresses.

Most of us are willing to put ourselves out to a remarkable degree for the people we like, respect and trust. If you can build that relationship with each team member, then you have a resource that will be committed to your project and go the extra mile when times get tough, not just because it's their job, nor even because of what the project can accomplish, but because you ask them to. That is real leadership.

Team roles

Each person brings three things to the team:

1 Their skills, expertise and knowledge

2 Their personality, character and style

3 Their preferred team role.

As mentioned in Chapter 1, the best-known study of the roles we play in teams was conducted by Meredith Belbin in the 1970s. His work has led to a set of popular and valuable team-role survey tools that help team members and leaders understand how each team member likes to contribute to their team and what the resulting balance or imbalance means for team performance.

All of the team-role models available (the other widely used one was developed by Charles Margerison and Dick McCann) emphasise that what is important in a team is that all roles are filled and balanced. In small teams, people can fill more than one role.

We each have role preferences. In some of us there are one or two really strong preferences and in others there is a more even balance. Our role preferences change as we gain new experiences and fit into new contexts. Where you spot a gap in the role preferences of your team, you will need to ask someone with this as a secondary preference to step in and fill it. Likewise, where two or more team members have a matching strong preference, there is scope for conflict unless you can find a way to harness both team members' preferences.

We will illustrate the nature of team roles with a quick introduction to Belbin's model and, for further information, refer you to the proprietary materials for any of the widely used models, such as *Team Roles at Work* by R. Meredith Belbin.

In his book, Belbin has identified nine team roles.

1 **Coordinator**
Likes to motivate and lead a team by drawing in all contributions

2 **Shaper**
Likes to take control and challenge others to perform well – particularly under pressure

3 **Plant**
Creative and unorthodox, Plants have loads of ideas and thrive on problem solving

4 **Team worker**
Wants the team to work together harmoniously and likes to listen, conciliate and socialise

5 **Implementer**
Wants to focus on getting the job done efficiently and effectively

6 **Monitor-evaluator**
Likes to get decisions right and ensure things meet either external or internal standards

7 **Resource investigator**
Good at making contacts, building relationships and accessing the resources the team needs

8 **Completer-finisher**
Feels a strong need to get things finished on time and to specification

9 **Specialist**
Has a primary focus on developing and using their specialist skills and knowledge.

As you can probably see, we all have a bit of each, but we perform best when we are in a role that allows us to exercise our preferences.

Stretching each person

When you ask me to do something I am familiar with, and have done a number of times before, it is easy for me; I am in my 'comfort zone'. I won't learn much doing the task, and can easily get bored. If it's too easy, I can even slip into a zone of complacency, where I no longer think about what I am doing, so could readily make mistakes. In a hazardous environment, the 'complacency zone' is a high-risk place to be.

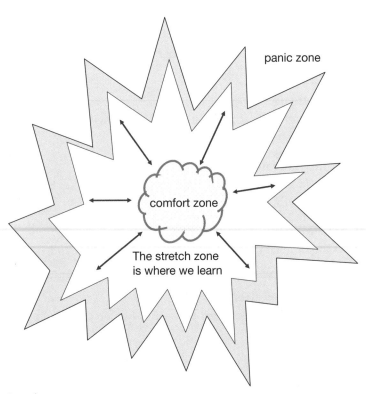

panic zone

comfort zone

The stretch zone is where we learn

Stretch zone

On the other hand, if you ask too much of me, with inadequate preparation or support, I am liable to feel stressed or even panicked by the task. I may or may not succeed, but the adrenalin will leave me exhausted and unable to learn fully from my experience. Between this 'panic zone' and the comfort zone lies the place where learning and development happen easily. We call it the 'stretch zone'.

Your role as leader is to take every opportunity to stretch team members, so that they are stimulated and they learn. When we feel stretched, and we have a clear understanding of what is expected of us, and we can also monitor our performance, we have the perfect conditions for what is known as '*flow*'. Flow is the mental state where we can concentrate effortlessly – sometimes for hours on end. We are entirely focused on what we are doing and find the experience rich and rewarding. At the end of a flow state we feel a sense of accomplishment and growth in our capabilities.

There are five leadership skills that will help you stretch people in this way.

1. Listening

The greatest gift that you can give someone is your undivided attention, so here is a simple three-step process for really listening well.

Step 1: Turn off the little voice in your own head

If you are listening to your own thoughts, then you can't be listening to me with all of your attention. We all do it, of course: as soon as I start speaking, you start to think of your response. Instead, listen to me, and don't be afraid of the little silence at the end while you frame your response. The silence will tell me you really listened, and your response will be to what I said, rather than to what you thought I was going to say when I started speaking.

Step 2: Suspend your judgement

I know you have your own values, beliefs, ideas and prejudices. But if you filter what I say through them, you will never really hear what my ideas mean to me, and how I feel about the challenges I am under. Listen to me without judgement, and then add your own point of view later, if it becomes relevant to our conversation.

Step 3: Pay attention to your listening

Check how well you are listening. If you hear that little voice in your head, turn it down and tune in to me again. If you feel yourself judging me, then suspend it and listen to what I am telling you first. If you catch your attention wandering, bring it back to me. One simple tip to improve your listening is to make sure that your whole body is turned towards me.

2. Goal setting

People need to know what you expect of them: this is the purpose of goal setting. It forms a kind of 'mini-contract' between you and them, so the terms must be clear. Ensure that the goal has a clear statement of what a good outcome, good performance, or the right behaviour looks like to create a sound basis for me to monitor what I am doing and to act as a sound basis for your feedback. You may want to write it down, but this is seldom necessary and may be insulting, unless it is a part of an organisational process.

What a lot of people forget is that a performance goal needs explicit agreement from both parties. I need to agree to accept the goal and you need to agree that, in meeting it, I will have done something worthwhile. You may also want to agree details like reporting, supervision and support.

3. Feedback

Good feedback is what turns a goal into an opportunity for real growth. In the early 1980s, researchers Albert Bandura and Daniel Cervone discovered that students given performance goals and regular feedback considerably outperformed similar students given just goals, just feedback, or neither. There are more details in *Brilliant Time Management*.

Design your feedback to give people a real BOOST.

 **brilliant** tool

Feedback to give a performance BOOST

Balanced   Don't just criticise: tell me what I have done well.
Don't just praise me: tell me how I can do better.
If I really achieved perfection, tell me. Then tell me what the next challenge could be.

Observed   Base your feedback on direct evidence, ideally on things you have observed directly, or on data and facts. If you must rely on reported observations, then take care to test them out first.

Objective   Keep your feedback to performance and behaviour. Your role is not to give me feedback on 'me'. So, 'You didn't do a good job with ...' is okay, but 'You are not very good at ...' is inappropriate, because you can't possibly know that for sure. There may be many reasons why I did a poor job.

Specific   The more specific you are with your feedback, the easier it will be for me to address it, and hone my skills. So 'This report is not satisfactory' won't help me make it better, but 'The tables in section 2 are not consistent with your comments, and I don't find your arguments for your conclusion compelling' will. I might ask 'Can you be more specific about my arguments?'

Timely   Usually, the sooner you give feedback, the better. The exception is when there is a good reason to delay. Examples might be: you want to see if I can figure out what I have done wrong for myself, it may be inappropriately overheard, or there is too much time pressure.

4. Reprimands

Going beyond feedback, you may occasionally need to reprimand a team member for inappropriate behaviours. As with objective feedback, always reprimand the behaviour, rather than the person, and be specific about what they did wrong and why it was inappropriate. Then show your support for the person and let them know that a single event will not affect your regard for them – assuming their behaviour did not step over a line.

brilliant example

It is important to know when a reprimand is not needed: people know when they have made mistakes. One particularly brilliant project leader was Sir Ernest Shackleton. One of the surgeons on his *Endurance* crew saw what happened when two men got a wire rope tangled around the ship's propeller. He said of Shackleton:

'There were no recriminations at all. The thing was done and the thing was to get it undone.'

This was always Shackleton's way: to recognise that there is nothing to be gained by recriminations and everything to be gained by getting on and fixing things.

Sometimes, in the heat of the moment, and in the cloud of uncertainty that envelops some projects, you will make a mistake and reprimand somebody unnecessarily, settle on the wrong person, or make your reprimand unduly severe. Do not hesitate to own up to your mistake and personally apologise to that person as soon as you can.

5. Coaching

Listening, goal setting and feedback are all components of a coaching style of leading and developing people. Coaching has

become an essential tool for leaders at all levels in most busi-
nesses and organisations. The fundamentals of a coaching style
are: first, to create an awareness and understanding of the situation in the person you are coaching; second, to help them choose
an appropriate course of action for themselves; and finally, to
encourage them to take responsibility for their choice and for
their subsequent actions. In a later conversation, you help them
to understand fully the consequences of their choice and the
actions they actually took as a consequence, so that they can
learn and make the next step.

The most popular model for coaching at work is the GROW
ME model, which is well described in John Whitmore's excellent
book, *Coaching for Performance*.

Goals	The coach supports the learner in identifying a clear performance goal.
Reality	The coach helps the learner assess accurately the evidence for their performance, the situation's requirements, and the resources available.
Options	The coach will encourage the learner to find as many options for improving performance or achieving their goal as possible, and then assist them in evaluating those options objectively, against the evidence from the reality stage.
Will	The coach compels the learner to make a choice of what option or options they will pursue and agrees a commitment for their future actions.
Monitor and evaluate	The coach will monitor and evaluate the learner's performance against the commitment they made at the will stage.

Inspiring and motivating people

Good listening and coaching will be motivating in themselves, but there is plenty more that you can do to inspire and motivate

> you need to find the separate key that will unlock each individual's motivation

team members. The important thing to remember here is not to swallow any 'motivation theory' whole. Everyone is different and you need to find the separate key that will unlock each individual's motivation.

The basics

Start by taking care of the basics: the hygiene factors. People will never be motivated if they don't feel secure in their role, that they are being treated fairly, offered reasonable challenges, rewarded appropriately, and given reasonable working conditions and the tools to do their job. Attend to grievances and conflicts quickly and fairly. This is basic management.

Inspire

Inspire people with your passion and enthusiasm for your project and find ways to communicate them in compelling and powerful ways. We will return to this in Chapter 5.

Boost

The best boost that you can give your people is to give them the self-confidence to perform at their best, free from unnecessary fears of criticism. This means demonstrating your trust in them and maintaining an optimism that the team's efforts will be repaid with success. This is not a blind trust or foolish optimism. Temper trust with careful risk-assessment and take appropriate steps to manage the risks you find. Involve individuals in the risk-assessment process and in designing mitigation and contingency strategies for their work areas.

Recognise

Recognition is one of the best ways to motivate colleagues. Acknowledge even small successes, say 'Well done', and offer the reward of a thank you. We will see how important celebrating team successes can be, but it is equally important to celebrate individual successes. When you do this, remember to put them in the context of the team's goal, so that everyone can see that it benefits them.

There's one more individual: you

If the first essential component of project leadership is the individuals, don't forget that you too are an individual; let your individuality show. The worst thing you can do is force yourself to fit in with your team or your organisation in ways that are uncomfortable. Be true to yourself and your colleagues will respect you for who you are.

Be yourself

One of the most valuable aspects of yourself to let show is your sense of humour. Don't confuse a solemn workplace with a serious one. People like smiling and humour because these reflect an inner confidence in yourself and your endeavours. Also let people know something of who you are away from your project. This is not about revealing all of your personal life, but some element of your interests which will show colleagues what makes you 'you'.

Your leadership point of view

What fundamentally makes you 'you' are your values and beliefs. We'll talk in Chapter 6 about how to articulate your message in a compelling, persuasive and powerful way, but first you have to articulate your own leadership point of view.

Now is the time to articulate it for yourself. When writing down your thoughts, think about how you will appeal to each team member's head, heart and gut.

Head: Do you offer a logical perspective that makes sense and accords with the facts?

Heart: Do you hook team members at an emotional level, to create a feeling of passion and commitment?

Gut: Does your point of view feel right? If it doesn't, people won't follow you unreservedly, no matter how much their head and heart tell them to.

brilliant exercise

Develop your own leadership point of view. Write down your answers to these four questions.

Observation: What are the most important things about your project?

Assertion: What does this really mean for you and your team? These may be challenges, rewards, threats, consequences or a combination.

Beliefs: What do you really believe about your team, your project or yourself? These are the most important things to you, in the context of your project and your team. Think of this as your manifesto statement.

Invitation: What are the consequences of your observation, assertion and beliefs? What do you want people to do as a result? This is your invitation to commit: your call to action.

Personal example

This will all come to nothing unless you can set a personal example that endorses your point of view. That is what integrity is all about. You must be as prepared to share in your team's pains as in their triumphs.

> You must be as prepared to share in your team's pains as in their triumphs.

You must be prepared to accept all of the blame and give all of the credit to your team, because only one thing measures your success as a leader: the success of your team.

▶ brilliant example

Steve came into work one day with a diary full of meetings and reports. He was going to be very busy. But he arrived to find the yard snow-bound, and the first arrivals among his team starting to clear it with shovels, brooms and anything they could find. Without taking his coat off, he went up to the colleague who seemed to be prioritising the clearance and said 'What do you want me to do?' Steve didn't go to his desk until the yard was clear. When he did, it was just to take off his coat, before heading to the canteen and buying soup and sandwiches for everyone who had been out there. He was very pleased to be invited to join them while they ate and drank.

Brilliant project behaviours

Integrity is, of course, top of the list of brilliant project behaviours! It's an attitude that manifests itself in every decision you make and everything you do.

The simple things count for a lot. Smiling and showing your confidence and optimism are important: they boost morale and help the least confident team members know it is going to be okay. So too is honesty: share your concerns about the reality of the situation, or your optimism will seem false, because people will fill any gap in your communication with rumours and speculation.

Be generous and supportive to each member of your team, treating them all with respect and giving everyone an equal chance to succeed, develop and shine.

Finally, focus on your project's outcomes and be passionate about them every day.

 brilliant recap

- Value each team member as an individual, for who they are and what they can contribute.

- Understand the importance of team roles and balance your team accordingly.

- Stretch your team members to give them opportunities to learn and develop. Cultivate the skills of listening, goal setting, feedback and coaching.

- Inspire and motivate team members by hooking onto each person's individual motivations.

- Be yourself and articulate your own leadership point of view.

CHAPTER 3

Build and share a clear plan

A stranger arrived in a foreign land, a mysterious woman dressed in a cape, her face hidden from the strong sunshine. She came across some men working. There she stopped and enquired of the first man, who was surrounded by stones and rubble: 'What are you doing?' He replied: 'I am putting stones on top of each other.'

She came across a second worker, surrounded by stones and rubble. Again she asked: 'What are you doing?' He replied: 'I am building a wall.'

As she came to a third worker, surrounded by stones and rubble, she put the same question to him: 'What are you doing?' He replied: 'I am building a library.'

And to a fourth worker, surrounded by stones and rubble, she again asked the same question: 'What are you doing?' He replied: 'I am building a home for all of the knowledge and wisdom of mankind'.

Humans have a deep need for meaning in our lives, and one of the roles of leadership is to put mundane things into a context that gives them meaning. In organisational projects, there is a hierarchy of meaning just like that in the story.

The diagram overleaf illustrates this nicely. At the top of an organisation is a 'mission statement' describing what the organisation exists for. From this, senior executives devise a direction in which to take the organisation, and call it a 'strategy'. From the strategy, managers devise a 'plan' for how to move the organisation in that direction. Following that plan, project leaders and team members do the hard work of getting things done.

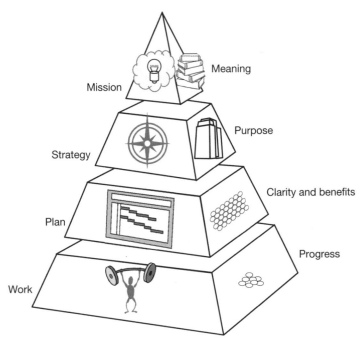

Pyramid of meaning

Moving back up, at the bottom of the pyramid, workers need to see progress: stones piled on top of one another. They also need clarity – to see what is expected of them and what the benefits are: a wall. More fundamentally, we need a purpose in life – to create things: a library. But deepest in our soul is a need for meaning; why are we doing this? We need to create value around us and benefit society: gathering knowledge and wisdom.

The project planning hierarchy

Planning your project will create a hierarchy of components called GOSPA:

Goal   What your project is designed to achieve

Objectives The criteria against which your project's success
                will be measured

Strategy   The broad approach you will take to achieving
                your goal and objectives

Plan   Details of how to attain your objectives: time,
                tasks and resources

Activities Getting the day-to-day tasks done.

All of these levels are equally important, but we start at the top and work our way down, each level guiding the development of the one below it. As project leader, your responsibilities are:

● To ensure that the goal is clearly articulated and will benefit the organisation or its clients

● To generate consistent and achievable objectives that will allow the project to be evaluated

● To use this basis to come up with a strategy to deliver the project

● To focus on the details necessary to derive a robust and realistic plan for what needs to be done, how you will deploy your resources, and how you will schedule activities to meet your objectives

● To allocate activities to team members in such a way that your project succeeds and your team members benefit from their involvement

● To achieve a balance between a clear sight of the project goal and a day-to-day focus on near-term activities.

Chapters 6 and 7 will focus on the detailed leadership tasks in developing your goal and objectives, and your strategy and plan.

Involve your team in preparing their plan

A shared goal and objectives will unite your team, but even better is for them to participate in creating it. You have a choice of leadership approaches for developing a project plan, which vary from telling team members your plan, through selling it to them, consulting them on how it should look, to handing over the planning process and letting them create it.

This continuum of leadership styles was first articulated by Robert Tannenbaum and Warren Schmidt in the late 1950s, and is illustrated below.

Continuum of leadership behaviour:
Seven degrees of management authority and team-member freedom

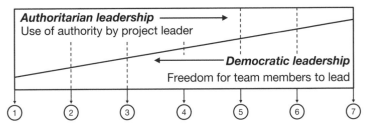

Continuum of leadership behaviours

What style you use will depend on three things:

You: Your values and personal style, and your
                    assessment of the risk

Your team: Your assessment of their readiness and
                    enthusiasm to assume responsibility

The project: Time pressure, the group's effectiveness,
                    organisational culture and the nature of the
                    project.

Tannenbaum and Schmidt identified seven distinct leadership behaviours.

1. Project leader creates the plan and announces it

This is an authoritarian style in which you give your team no opportunity to participate and give little or no consideration to their points of view. This is most appropriate in a crisis, where you need to give clear instructions.

2. Project leader 'sells' their plan

Here too, you create the plan yourself but, to limit resistance, you advocate its benefits to the group. This is valuable when your plan is not for debate, but you need the team's support.

3. Project leader presents their plan and invites questions

Once again, you are in control, but now you let the team explore your ideas to better understand the plan. Use this approach when you want to show yourself to be accountable to your team, but without committing to take account of their opinions.

4. Project leader presents a draft plan, subject to change

Now your team's opinions can count. You retain the role of building the plan, but consult your team before finalising it. This approach is most valuable when your team has valuable contributions to make, but you need to keep ultimate decision-making authority.

5. Project leader presents the goal and objectives, gets suggestions and then builds a plan

As before, you retain ultimate planning authority, but now you share responsibility for creating it with the team. Help them to feel able to make suggestions that will really influence the final plan, and approach your team with an open mind, to capitalise on their knowledge and insights. Steer the process gently. Use this approach when you want to harness the full range of knowledge and ideas that your team has.

6. Project leader defines the limits within which the group builds the plan

Now planning sits with the team. You retain responsibility for defining the goal and objectives and, significantly, setting boundaries within which the team can plan. This is delegation, although you may wish to be a part of the planning process. In this case, do not seek any disproportionate influence; let a team member steer the process. Take this approach when your team has all of the skills needed to do the planning, but you have a clear idea of some parameters that you want them to work within.

7. Project leader allows group to create the plan, subject to organisational constraints

Give your team as much freedom as you can: any limits come from a higher level. Again, you may assist the team and again, respect the decisions the team arrives at. This is the best approach when you have confidence in your team's commitment and expertise, and want them to feel that confidence.

Communicate your plan

Whichever style of leadership you adopt in creating a plan, you absolutely must communicate it effectively, so that every team member has a comprehensive understanding of the big picture and how it affects them and their future workload. The better informed people are, the better able they will be to carry out their duties, to innovate, and to take the initiative.

> The better informed people are, the better able they will be to carry out their duties

brilliant tip

Ten ways to communicate your plan

1   Team meeting

2   Mini-conference with presentations

3   Show and tell session with sub-teams describing their parts of a plan

4   One-to-one or small group briefings

5   Printed planning documents

6   Wall posters

7   Intranet or shared file space

8   Online or hosted project management collaboration tools (such as Basecamp, Backpack, Zoho Projects, eRoom or Huddle)

9   Video and rich media

10   Create a newsletter or project magazine.

Needless to say, the best approach is to combine more than one of these.

Tailor your plan to each individual

Your plan will address people's need for certainty. Without the plan, their lack of certainty will damage their confidence in you. However, people also have a need for flexibility and if the plan is too rigid, they can feel stifled.

As you roll out your plan, it is important to adapt it to each individual on your team. For example, Mairead may like a lot of autonomy, so keep the elements of the plan that concern her work at a high level, whilst for Max, who likes to know precisely what is expected of him, you should plan in more detail.

Situational leadership

Situational leadership is an approach that adapts your leadership style to the situation you are dealing with at the moment. The seven leadership styles that we saw for how to develop a plan are an example of situational leadership. In implementing your plan and allocating work to individuals, it is easier to work with a simpler model. Here are four examples of different situations and how you could deal with them.

Instructing Ilya

Your team is working hard to complete a deliverable by the end of the month. Ilya has recently joined the team and must contribute a detailed piece of analysis by next Friday. He is eager to learn but has never done this kind of analysis.

His lack of knowledge means Ilya needs some clear instructions, but he is eager to learn, so once you have broken the task down and given him guidance on the first chunk, leave him to it and ask him to check with you when it is done, or come to you if he gets stuck. Check on him from time to time.

Persuading Paloma

Paloma is bored and thinks her role is pointless. She is inexperienced and does not fully understand what she needs to do or how to tackle it.

Give careful feedback on Paloma's performance and explain how it fits into the wider project. Because she is inexperienced, show her what she needs to accomplish and ask her how she could tackle it. Help her decide on a way forward, offer her encouragement to boost her enthusiasm, and check on her progress frequently.

Assisting Adnan

Adnan has a great track record, but recently suffered some big setbacks for reasons beyond his control. Now his morale is low and his performance has dropped right down.

Adnan is clearly capable, so you don't need to tell him what to do, but you do need to be supportive, to rebuild his morale. So discuss his recent setbacks with him, listen to how he feels about the project and help him explore ways to get back on top. Stop by and have a chat with him periodically and be supportive if he is still encountering problems.

Trusting Emiko

You have asked Emiko to lead a highly sensitive consultation. She is very capable, is sensitive to how her colleagues feel, and has led important pieces of work successfully in the past. She is keen to get started.

Tell Emiko the objectives of the consultation and ask her to keep you updated on progress. You don't need to offer any more advice, or it will suggest you don't trust her to do what she knows she is good at and will therefore demotivate her. Her enthusiasm means she does not need your support; she just needs to know you are there if she has a problem.

How it works

In each of these cases, you should be assessing two things: your team member's ability to do the work at hand and how they feel about the task: are they confident and motivated or nervous and hesitant?

The more able they are, the less you need to instruct them. Beginners need a step-by-step guide to ensure that they stay within their stretch zone and, importantly, stay safe. Skilled experts need no guidance at all.

The less confident and enthusiastic your team member is, the more you need to actively support them, to supplement their confidence and motivation, and keep them from the panic zone.

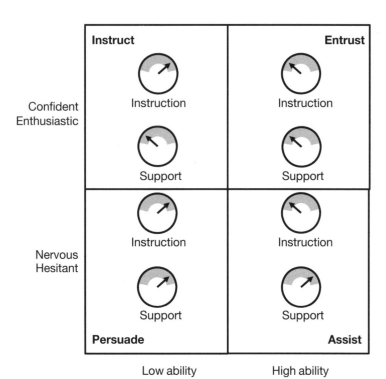

Support and instruction

By tailoring the amount of instruction and support you give each person in each situation, you will be able to lead everybody in the way they need and want.

A brilliant plan

A brilliant project is one that matters. That means that people can attach a positive emotion to its purpose; they can see it as bringing about worthwhile change. We'll see more about how to communicate this in Chapter 5. In this chapter, you have read about how to connect your project – and the individual activities within it – to a higher meaning, up through the hierarchy. Make this evident to your team and to the people involved in the project in other ways. Stating a powerful and compelling goal is one way to make this meaning evident.

The other factor in creating a brilliant plan is to make it directly relevant to each team member, by adapting the amount of instruction and detail to their individual needs. This way, each person will see the plan as one with which they can thrive and develop.

 brilliant recap

- We all have a need for meaning in our lives and projects are part of a pyramid of meaning from your organisation's mission down to how your project can create the change that is needed.

- Use the GOSPA framework to put together a plan that your team can rally around.

- Involve your team in preparing the plan and communicate the finished plan thoroughly.

- Tailor the components of your plan to the people who will carry it out.

CHAPTER 4

Foster a true sense of team spirit

H ave you ever been part of a team that exceeded every-body's expectations, and was also a joy to be a part of? Your colleagues may not have been your best friends, but you respected and liked them. Work just got done and you all felt you achieved great things. This is a 'high-performing team'. This chapter is about creating the conditions that foster this spirit.

brilliant exercise

There is no simple definition of a high-performing team, but you can create your own, as well as your own action list to create one. Look at this list of words, and mark any that fit your sense of what you want most from a high-performing team. Second, highlight the top three which you feel are your priorities to work on with your own team.

☐ Capability	☐ Care	☐ Complementarity
☐ Commitment	☐ Continuity	☐ Charisma
☐ Collaboration	☐ Confidence	☐ Common sense
☐ Conscience	☐ Communication	☐ Character
☐ Cheerfulness	☐ Consideration	☐ Candour
☐ Contribution	☐ Catalyst	☐ Cohesion

▶

☐ Captain/Chief	☐ Compassion	☐ Clarity
☐ Culture	☐ Capacity	☐ Consistency
☐ Compatibility	☐ Cooperation	☐ Calm
☐ Creativity	☐ Challenge	☐ Cool
☐ Constructive	☐ Control	☐ Chilled
☐ Conscientious	☐ Community	☐ Courage
☐ Civility	☐ Competence	☐ Contentment
☐ Coaching	☐ Customer focus	☐ Coordination
☐ Calculating	☐ Congratulation	☐ Collective responsibility
☐ Collegiate	☐ Celebration	

This exercise will help you to understand what a high-performing team means in your domain, and to prioritise the steps you can take to move your team in that direction.

Team culture

A team will develop a culture of its own, whether you help it to or not. If you do not actively guide the culture, you may not like what you find. Once a culture is formed, it can be hard to change, so it is far better to work from the outset on developing the team culture that you want.

Culture can mean anything from work patterns and behaviours to ethics and morality. It is one of the hardest words in the English language to define. Perhaps the most noticeable feature will be the working atmosphere the team creates around itself.

As project leader, it is your behaviours and approach that will set the tone for the team's style and culture. People will assume that what you do and how you do things are 'all right', and so will start to mimic them, assuming your patterns of behaviour are what you want to

> it pays to be aware of the tone you set

see in them. You cannot *not* influence your team in this way; so it pays to be aware of the tone you set from day one.

Agreed ways of working

You may want to develop some agreed ways of working among your team. These things extend from informal or even formal working rules, such as working hours and breaks, to the sorts of things that will become team rituals and traditions, like 'We always go out for a drink together after work, on the final Friday of the month' or 'We always get together for fifteen minutes on a Monday morning for a progress update ... and someone always brings doughnuts.'

Many of these will evolve over the course of your project: most of them organically. Don't feel you need to initiate much of this, but do pick up on helpful ideas and help the team turn them into traditions. Where you might usefully take the lead is in setting the tone for how your team tackles its most difficult challenges, such as problem solving or handling conflict, as well as more formal elements, like how you conduct team meetings. We will examine team meetings and conflict in the next chapter, so let's use problem solving as a quick example.

Here are two examples of how different project leaders handle problem solving. Both are effective for their teams, and both trigger a comforting sense of 'We've done it this way before, and it works' whilst remaining completely flexible.

 **example**

Goran's contact book

When a team member comes to Goran with a problem, if at all possible he will drop everything else and give it his full attention. He will sit down with his colleague and talk it over with them. Sometimes a solution will emerge, or an obvious next step. If one doesn't, Goran nearly always says 'Leave it with me' and goes back to his desk to look through his extensive list of contacts. Very quickly, he will identify one or two 'experts' whom he can bring into the project to work with his team members and create a solution. People love the stimulation and challenge of these new people and the ideas they bring, and have come almost to welcome problems!

Neeta's sessions

When a team member brings a problem to Neeta, she asks a few simple questions about the nature of the problem, and its urgency. If no resolution strikes either of them, Neeta will often say 'Sounds like we need a session.' She will suggest two or three team members who might be helpful in solving the problem, and ask her colleague to suggest some too. They will discuss names and select three or four people, then call a meeting to work on the problem, which Neeta may or may not attend. When she does, she always lets someone else take the lead, only stepping in if an important decision is needed, for which she feels she needs to take responsibility.

Ambiguity is disastrous

People like variety and flexibility but too much ambiguity is dangerous for a team, some of whose members will find it too unsettling. Work on getting the team's 'hygiene factors' like working hours, breaks, handovers of work and meetings 'right' for your team, so that they feel that they will succeed or fail as one team, and that nothing other than their own performance will get in their way.

Sometimes you may want to take a more structured approach, and introduce a set of formal ground rules, or even a 'team charter'.

Formal ground rules

Ground rules set up an agreement about how the team wants to work together. Most often, they are unwritten, but some project leaders like to use their first meeting to facilitate a set of ground rules that everyone is comfortable with, and record them on a board. They will then transcribe these as a record for the team.

---

brilliant example

Here are some example ground rules contributed by different project teams.

- We don't talk badly about our project outside the team.
- It's okay to leave at five if your work is done.
- We will make time to mark and celebrate all major milestones.
- No ideas are stupid ideas.
- Meetings always start on time – it's your responsibility to be there.
- Family comes first.
- We offer to help each other when our own work is done.
- Morning meetings end by 9.30.

These sort of ground rules can establish a 'psychological contract' between team members that sets the boundaries of acceptable behaviour. The more explicit you make them, the more they move to what is known as a 'team charter', which is usually a written set of ground rules that the team expects everyone to accept. This can also define the relationship between the team and the organisation as a whole, or other teams within it.

There are advantages and disadvantages to a more formal approach. It may be seen by some as giving more security, but by others as being more constraining. If you do create a charter, it must be consistent with the prevailing culture of your wider organisation and needs commitment from all sides. Its primary value may be symbolic and if this is so, do not try to enforce it too strictly. Instead, use it as a set of guiding principles to clarify expectations and interpret conflict.

The three Rs

There are three things that most people value above all in the workplace: respect, recognition and relationships. You must prioritise each of these in the way you lead your team. Let's consider them in turn.

Respect

People need to feel that they are respected by all of their colleagues. One way to emphasise your commitment in this area is to make courtesy a personal priority, and to expect it of team members. Another is to celebrate the diversity of your team and make sure everybody listens equally to all ideas and values every contribution.

> A major component of respect is the integrity with which you treat people

A major component of respect is the integrity with which you treat people. Professor Roderick Kramer is an expert on trust in organisations and asserts that keeping your promises has the biggest impact of any action you can take. It is far more important than expensive methods like away-days with their sometimes complex trust-building exercises.

One 'R' that you may think is missing is responsibility. However, I include this with respect – have enough respect for me to give me the responsibility I have earned. This too will build deep trust.

Recognition

... or reward?

What people really value is recognition. Reward is just one form of recognition and, at the time of writing this book, there is a lot of coverage in the serious and scientific press about research showing that bonuses, in white-collar roles, have the perverse-seeming effect of undermining performance. However, if you recognise the contribution I have made, then I too will credit that achievement. It will help me feel valued, and give my confidence a real boost.

However, when you recognise a particularly significant achievement, there is no harm in a suitable reward. The best rewards are celebrations of achievement. Whether we are celebrating individual or team performance, a celebration can involve the whole team and further bring it together.

Relationships

Many people spend over half of their waking hours in the workplace. So it should come as no surprise how important relationships with our colleagues are. Good humour and opportunities for social exchanges within and outside the project will strengthen relationships, trust and understanding, and hence improve performance.

Team-building techniques

Here is a checklist of ten things you can do to strengthen your team.

1. Training opportunities

Use training as a way to bring your team together. You can use formal training courses, seminars, cross-training (where team members train colleagues in some of their skills and expertise), show-and-tell sessions or any format where team members can work together and share knowledge.

2. Team meetings

You will need to have team meetings, so use them as an opportunity to develop your team. Celebrate achievements, share lessons learned, recognise innovations, collaborate on problem solving, introduce an element of fun. Give some of your meetings a theme.

3. Social events

If your team can spend time together outside the project environment, the relationships will get stronger. Adopt a variety of different types of event that suit the preferences of team members, but make sure that none of the formats deliberately excludes any members.

4. Be generous with credit

When people do well, tell them, and tell others. When the team does well, share the credit out. When you do well, credit your team. But hoard the blame to yourself. You must believe in your team and if they do foul up, give them the confidence that you know they can and will get it right next time.

5. Link team members together

In the early days particularly, an important part of your role is to get to know each individual so that you can link together team members to collaborate. Once they get to know each other, most of your linking role will focus on bringing in external people to contribute to or critique your project.

6. Lay the groundwork to hand over control to your team

The highest-performing teams are self-managing and your role will be a background role of maintaining the environment in which they can thrive, and the flow of resources they need, whilst shielding them from unneeded interruptions. Like a good parent, you will have done a good job when your team can take care of themselves and

> you will have done a good job when your team can take care of themselves

they no longer need you – except for the odd cash injection!

7. Away-days and team building

Views on these are mixed, from evangelical fervour (and not just among the vendors) to outright cynicism. As always, there is something in every perspective, but the truth is more subtle. Plan away-days and team-building events with great care and they will deliver real value. Scrimp on the planning and they will fail appallingly and possibly destroy any team coherence you already have.

brilliant dos and don'ts

Away-days and team building

Do

✔ Start by knowing what you want to achieve.

✔ Plan carefully.

✔ Review the health and safety and accessibility implications.

✔ Visit any centre you are using and meet the consultants.

✔ Ensure that people know why you are doing it.

✔ Remind people that they are still representing your organisation and that behaviours still matter.

✔ Build in unstructured social time.

Don't

✘ Impose physical challenges on the unwilling.

✘ Create an event just for the sake of it, or think of it as a 'freebie' – it has to produce justifiable results.

▶

✗   Choose any activity that will make your colleagues feel deeply uncomfortable.

✗   Allow the event to become more important than your project.

8. Make conspicuous commitments

Making real commitments on behalf of your team can give them a real pressure to perform and energise them. But do be careful that the commitments you make, while stretching, are reasonable, otherwise you will cause resentment.

9. Name your team

A name gives a team a sense of identity, so give serious consideration to naming your team, or inviting the team to come up with their own name. The best names reflect either what the team is trying to achieve or the spirit and style with which it wants to work. You will find more information on this at the start of Chapter 6.

brilliant example

Here is a list of team names, as chosen by contestants in the TV series *The Apprentice*, in both the UK and the United States. Some will seem corny or inappropriate; others may appeal. Just thinking through which ones you hate and which you like, and why, may give you some good ideas.

Alpha	Capital Edge	Gold Rush
Apex	Eclipse	Hydra
Apollo	Empire	Ignite
Arrow	Excel	Impact
Athena	First Forté	Impresario

Instinct	Mosaic	Synergy
Invicta	Net Worth	Velocity
Kinetic	Protégé	Venture
Kotu	Renaissance	Versacorp
Logic	Revolution	
Magna	Stealth	

See if you can guess which were chosen by men's teams and which by women, and which come from the US show and which from the British version. To find out, go to www.brilliantprojectleader.co.uk.

10. Choose a deputy

You may not think you need a deputy – and you may be right. Ask yourself: what would happen if I were off sick for a month? Work through this scenario, possibly with a couple of team members, and then make your decision. Two apparently contradictory considerations should guide your choice (unless you work in a hierarchical environment, where your choice is evident).

First, choose somebody different from you, who thinks differently and gets different answers, and who has complementary skills and talents. If you choose someone just like you, then for most of the time, while you are present, they will add nothing to your thinking. Second, choose someone whose judgement you trust entirely. You will want sometimes to step away and feel confident that the leadership of your project is in safe hands.

Brilliant team

A brilliant team will be driven by a shared commitment to do real justice to your project. Give it the means to do this by providing it with the resources it needs, a clearly articulated goal, constant feedback on its progress, by sharing progress and informed comment from outsiders. Keep each individual and the team as a whole in their stretch zones, and give specific and spontaneous praise to the team as soon as it achieves a success or passes a notable milestone.

brilliant recap

- Create your own definition of a high-performing team, and determine what elements you most need to work on.

- Set the framework for the team culture that you want and then determine how much you wish to formalise it.

- Create an environment of respect, recognise contribution and help the team to develop and strengthen working relationships.

- Use as many means as are appropriate to build your team into a strong coherent unit that accepts a shared responsibility to succeed together.

CHAPTER 5

Communicate relentlessly – and well

There are two levels of leadership communication, linked to the pyramid of meaning you saw in Chapter 3. At the top of the pyramid, your communication needs to concentrate on articulating your vision for the project; its meaning in the wider context of your organisation or society. At the bottom of the pyramid, you focus on more practical, day-to-day issues like planning and getting things done. These two forms of communication are, respectively, 'Transformational' and 'Transactional' communication.

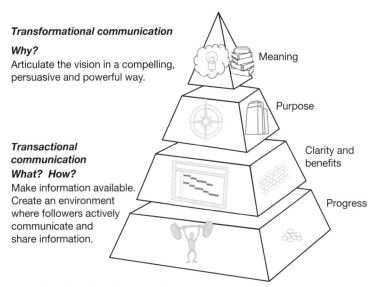

Transformational communication

Why?
Articulate the vision in a compelling, persuasive and powerful way.

Meaning

Purpose

Transactional communication
What? How?
Make information available. Create an environment where followers actively communicate and share information.

Clarity and benefits

Progress

Transformational and transactional communication

The role of transformational communication is to inspire people to commit to a change; to do something significant and perhaps difficult. To do this, you must answer the question 'Why?' with compelling and persuasive reasons.

Transactional communication is more mundane. It focuses on the 'What?' and the 'How?' of everyday project situations. Effective transactional communication must be easy to understand quickly, and unambiguous, allowing confident action in return.

In this chapter, we will examine three contexts for transactional communication: everyday team communication, project meetings and conflict; and also transformational communication that sets out a vision. We will also consider ways in which you can use technology to support team communication.

Team communication

There are three levels of project team communication: perhaps four if you want completeness. These mark the evolution of my own understanding of leading a project team. We'll start with the rather dubious 'fourth style', which I certainly observed in my early experiences as a team member, but never sought to emulate.

'Me-to-me'

Some project leaders like to keep their own counsel. They are either poor at communicating with their team, or they choose not to do so. As a result, team members feel constantly confused about what is going on and uncertain about what their project leader expects of them. It is uncomfortable for all and leads to blame and recriminations when things do not go according to the hidden plan.

'Me-to-team'

As a reaction to this style of leadership, I was determined, with my first project team, to communicate everything in an exemplary fashion. I went out of my way to keep my team informed of everything and they seemed to appreciate it. When confronted with problems, delays, unreasonable requirements from a client, or budget cuts, I had one rule.

Mike's first rule of communication

Honesty is not the best policy ...
... it is the only policy.

Sharing problems increases the team's intimacy and will harness the full range of skills that you have, to help solve them. When you understand what I want, and are well informed about the context, you are better able to make your own judgements and decisions, and act on your initiative. And because you are well informed, there is a good chance that your choices will be good ones.

So communicating well with your team does not only leave them feeling more positive, confident and empowered; it is, quite simply, a more efficient way to get your project done. A project leader's role is to provide information, data and facts to their team.

> communicating well with your team is a more efficient way to get your project done

'Team-to-me'

As I learned more about leading a team, I realised that 'Me-to-team' communication was not enough. Day to day, my team members were learning far more about their areas of the project than I was. For really good leadership, I needed to spend much of my time listening to them. This allowed me to undertake more sophisticated leadership activities, like:

- Acknowledging and praising success
- Being supportive through difficulties
- Assisting with problem solving and finding resources
- Disseminating good ideas
- Helping to avert risks and problems.

Listen more than you speak. One of the secrets of being a great project leader is to gather and apply other people's ideas. Do this on one condition, though: be generous with the credit for those ideas, or you will find that they start to dry up very quickly.

'Team-to-team'

Self-confidence is important for your team members, but increasingly I came to recognise the importance of self-confidence to the team as a whole. To create a self-confident team, I knew that I had to be able to step away, and that meant that really excellent team communication needs to happen spontaneously among team members, without any lead from the project leader.

Your role as project leader is to create an environment of trust where team members communicate among themselves, and make wise choices about how to do so. This means not using 'cc-all' emails for every single thing, but thinking about who needs to know what and how best to communicate each item. Each person must take full responsibility for their own communication and the team must have the confidence to resolve their own difficulties and conflicts for themselves. Your role becomes that of communicator of last resort, and link to the outside world.

Project meetings

Project meetings must be more than just a talking shop: they are chances to get work done, generate ideas, solve problems, evaluate options, make decisions and build relationships. Consequently, there is an infinity of possible formats and one of your responsibilities as project leader is to determine which will serve your project best at each stage, to see that they run effectively, and to keep the format under review, to ensure it remains fresh and appropriate to the shifting needs of your project.

We will look at a spectrum of meeting styles, and draw some lessons from each.

Team briefing

Team briefings are often the most formal style of meeting, in which one or a few people will convey information to the rest of the team. You may want little or no interaction; or a generous opportunity for participants to question or challenge the people leading the briefing. As it is a formal meeting, do take time to prepare it carefully and even consider rehearsing presentations. For large briefings to kick off a substantial project, this is a valuable investment in getting the tone right for your project and establishing a real sense of professionalism

If the subject of your briefing is controversial, it is also important to anticipate questions and challenges that you are likely to receive, and prepare well thought-out responses. A good way to do this is to ask a small number of trusted colleagues to attend a rehearsal of your presentation and then write down all of the questions and challenges they can think of. Build into your rehearsal a chance to test out your responses and find out how they sound to your trusted audience.

Supplement your team briefing by useful takeaway information so that people can focus on listening, rather than note-taking, but promise to give them the information at the end, rather than giving it out at the start, or they may just flick through and not listen to your presentation at all.

Formal team meeting

It is easy to get into a routine of formal team meetings and find that they rapidly achieve little, other than leave people feeling they could have spent their time better. To ensure that your meetings are truly worthwhile, manage them before, during and after the meeting, and do so with your meeting outcomes in mind. Here are some things you can do at each point, which together will help create meetings that team members will value, and which will deliver real results to your project.

Before your meeting: Preparation

Start your preparation as you would start any project: by thinking through your goal and what you want to achieve. Then mentally check whether a meeting is really the best way to do this and if so, what format to use. Once you have decided on a format, it is time to think about who to invite. Projects are busy environments, so only invite people who would have a good reason to be there, because they need to hear what is discussed in person, or because they can contribute to the discussion. Then determine the date, time and place that are most suitable.

You should be doing this with one-off meetings and with regular meetings, frequently reviewing their format, attendance and timing against what you want to use the meeting for at the current stage of your project.

Now is the time to prepare an agenda.

⚲ brilliant impact

A good agenda should have five elements:

1 A title that describes the purpose of the meeting.

2 A statement of the date, time and place.

3 A list of the outcomes you intend to achieve at the meeting – to really focus minds on why you are all there.

4 A list of topics to discuss. Against each topic should be the name of the person who will lead that discussion and the outcome you want from it, for example: informing, discussion, ideas, decision, or commitments for action.

5 A list of information or associated reading that attendees need to assimilate before the meeting. I would suggest separating this into required and supplementary reading. Set a rule that, if people don't come to the meeting properly prepared, then they do not stay. In return, you have a responsibility to keep the required reading material to the minimum necessary for attendees to understand and contribute to the meeting.

I also like to leave a space on printed agendas for a Parking lot. I discuss this further in the next subsection.

Once you have developed your agenda, decide what physical resources you will need for your meeting and make the arrangements for them: whiteboard, smart board, flip charts, projector, paper and pens, room layout and refreshments, or not.

Your choice of whether to have refreshments will depend a lot on personal preferences and your organisational culture. Some argue strongly it makes people comfortable and relaxed, so they can contribute freely. Others argue that the comfort and relaxation slow the meeting down and encourage waffling.

During your meeting: Effectiveness
Rule: Start on time. If you don't, and it becomes a habit, you are signalling that getting there on time is not important. I make a habit of arriving early and starting on time unless there is a known transport or project issue holding up a significant proportion of attendees. Give a strong signal to your team that, if you are late, they are to start without you and if you are absent, that the meeting should continue anyway. This is particularly so with regular team meetings.

If you do this, you are saying that it is a 'team' meeting, not 'your' meeting. It signals that the meeting is more important than your presence. You may want to assign some other specific roles to people at the meeting, rather than take them yourself.

brilliant tip

Seven meeting roles you may want to assign

● Note taker (to record what is said)

● Scribe (to record ideas and decisions on a board or flip chart)

● Facilitator (to conduct a discussion and draw in contributions from everyone)

● Critic (to challenge ideas, thinking critically, and play devil's advocate)

● Calculator (to evaluate ideas numerically, using the best available data)

● Researcher (to step out and secure extra information when needed)

● Monitor (to highlight conformity of ideas with mandatory standards, such as health and safety, or formal quality processes).

> You can use your formal meetings for a number of purposes

You can use your formal meetings – whether one-off or regular – for a number of purposes, and you will often combine them. You may want to cover: status review, lessons learned, problem sharing and resolution, risks and issues, decision making, successes and celebrations.

From time to time, topics will arise that are outside your agenda. You will need to decide whether to subvert your plan, because the topic is important and urgent enough to warrant it, or to note the topic and deal with it outside the meeting. If you do want to defer dealing with the topic (probably your default position), it is important to ensure that it is formally recorded, so that people to whom it is important know that it has been acknowledged and will be dealt with properly.

For this, I use a space on the board, or a flip chart sheet, headed 'Parking lot'. Whenever a topic arises that needs to be dealt with, but not here, not now, I conspicuously note it in the Parking lot and then move on quickly. I encourage attendees to also note it in their notebook or on their agenda. At the end of the meeting, I will quickly survey the Parking lot and ask, for each item, who will take the lead on either getting it resolved or calling a meeting to tackle it. I try and take on as few Parking lot items personally as possible.

After your meeting: Follow-up

Get minutes distributed quickly after the meeting – and definitely within 24 hours (not counting weekends). Keep them simple and action-focused.

 **tool**

Ideal project meeting minutes

Section 1: Commitments
Under each attendee's name, list the commitments they made for action and the deadlines they agreed.

Section 2: Decisions
List the decisions that were made at the meeting.

Section 3: Information and ideas
List the essential information and ideas that were shared at the meeting, or collated afterwards as a result of the meeting.

Section 4: Acknowledgements and celebration
Recognise and praise any contributions that arose during the meeting.

Project working-group meeting

A project working-group meeting is less formal than a team meeting and is often convened to solve a specific problem.

However, a useful approach on big complex projects is to convene a regular meeting to discuss and resolve emerging problems. Attendees may vary from meeting to meeting, although there would usually be a core group representing the primary aspects of the project, such as the technical areas, the major work streams, or the primary beneficiary groups.

At the start of the meeting, do a round-robin of the group, and record all of the issues that any participant wants to discuss. Invite each person to describe the issue succinctly: what is the issue and what are the potential consequences? When all of the issues are recorded, the next task is to prioritise these. Don't spend too long, so you may want to use a simple process. Examples include:

- Project leader chooses priority sequence
- Voting
- Discussion, then project leader interprets consensus
- Ranking A, B or C priority (A – must do at the meeting, B – would ideally do at the meeting, C – best left to outside the meeting).

Once you have your prioritised list, work through the topics in priority order and leave ten minutes at the end to decide how to tackle any topics that you have not got around to. This allows you to keep your meeting to a fixed time.

Morning stand-ups

Perhaps the most informal style of project meeting is to meet briefly each morning – or one or two mornings a week – and do a quick round-robin of status reports. Each person could contribute:

- what progress they have made since the last meeting
- what progress is planned by the next meeting
- issues or risks arising
- requests for help.

Keep these meetings quick and the number of contributors small. If you want the whole team to meet and it's a big team, ask for one report per subgroup. Alternatively, invite one representative from each work group, perhaps the work team leaders.

Dealing with conflict

Conflict may not be an inevitable part of a diverse team under pressure, but it is a likely consequence. If your team is mature and functions well, you may not need to intervene: they may resolve it for themselves. Otherwise, it is important to tackle it early, before it gets too hot.

Here are five strategies that can help.

1. One-to-one chats

Use informal conversations with the protagonists, offering feedback and advice. If you can engage with the dissenters early on, this is usually the only intervention you will need. Appeal to their commitment to the project, ascribe any bad behaviour to their enthusiasm, and help them find a way to repair any damage to their relationship.

2. Raising it in a team meeting

Deal with the issue publicly, but keep the discussion around the issue rather than the people. Revert to any team ground rules that you agreed early on, to keep the discussion positive and purposeful.

3. Mediation

Support the protagonists in resolving their dispute in a mediating role. Meet each one in advance to understand their perspectives, meet each again to explore areas for agreement and reconciliation. Then bring the protagonists together to agree a joint way forward, when there is enough common ground.

4. Confrontation

I have never had to resort to confronting team members in public, but it may be a choice you want to take. Prepare well by making sure you understand all of the facts and have thought through what you will say and how you will say it. Engage other team members in focusing the protagonists on the project and its goal, and use their peer pressure to highlight and deprecate bad behaviours. As always, be sure you can avoid the confrontation becoming personal.

> be sure you can avoid the confrontation becoming personal

5. Discipline

Your ultimate recourse is to discipline one or both parties. You may even need to make the decision to remove one or both from the project. These are extreme measures, so be sure that you can do this in a way that is manifestly fair, proportionate and aligned to your organisation's policies and procedures. Consider getting support from a more senior colleague.

In Chapter 10, you will learn a five-step process for resolving conflict, along with ten practical tips.

Articulate your vision

The transformational aspect of your team communication is all about sharing your vision for the project in a way that harnesses people's enthusiasm for a valued goal. Unlike transactional communication, you need to appeal not just to intellect, but to emotion. We make the choices we make for emotional reasons and then we justify those choices with logic and reason.

🡒 brilliant impact

Here are six ways to give your transformational communication some real impact.

1 Tell stories:	Use storytelling and metaphor to give your message real emotional depth.	
2 Focus on individuals:	When we talk about how something will affect dozens or hundreds or even thousands of people, it sounds good but has no emotional power. When you talk about the impact on a single person or family, it gives your message emotional resonance.	
3 Create pictures:	A vision is nothing if it does not conjure images in our minds, so use visual language that creates mental pictures.	
4 Portray movement:	What excites us is not 'What could be' but the gap between 'What could be' and 'What is'. Start with 'What is', and what is wrong with it, and then spell out a potential future.	
5 Build rhythm:	Return to 'What is' after showing a future, to create some yearning, and then return to the 'Could be', to show what is possible. Cycle back and forth to wear away resistance and build expectation.	
6 End on a crescendo:	A good ending will galvanise people. Use a call to action or a recap of the future to leave people feeling empowered and eager for change.	

Technology for team communications

For all of the technology that is available to you, nothing beats the personal touch of being there and talking to people individually and in small groups. But you may need to supplement this with additional modes. Perhaps the commonest, email, is also the worst: use it with great caution.

Text messaging contains arguably the least subtlety, but it does have the merit that the accepted convention is terseness. The problem with email is that we often write emails quickly and carelessly. But when we receive an email, we usually assume (often without thought) that it has been written carefully. For this reason, email frequently leads to miscommunication – sometimes of facts and ideas and often of mood and intent.

It may be foolish to even try to record all of the options for team communication given how rapidly they change and grow these days. Who would seriously recommend a printed memo in most organisations now? What is worth doing is to explore your options carefully, investing time and maybe money in one or two well-chosen tools, and then learn to use them really well.

 **brilliant** list

Top ten tools for project communication

1 Meetings

2 Cascade briefings (project leader briefs work-stream leaders, who brief team members)

3 Posters, notices, wallcharts

4 Video display panels and dashboards

5 Shared online or intranet workspace

6 Phone and phone conferencing (fixed line or internet technologies)

7 Video conferencing (fixed line or internet technologies)

8 Recorded messages (audio or video)

9 Websites, blogs and wikis

10 Text messaging or secure micro-blogging (like Twitter, but with only defined users, for example: present.ly or Communote).

Brilliant communication

The key to brilliant communication is the personal touch. The time commitment it involves communicates that it is important to you; it makes others feel valued.

Brilliant communication happens spontaneously. It happens when people talk and create a real buzz around what they are doing. They feel a desire to promote their project, because they share a passion for it. It is also planned. Thinking carefully about your message and how to relay it accurately and compellingly are essential to setting a positive tone.

Either way, brilliant communication is hard work. So communicate relentlessly, and communicate well.

 **brilliant** recap

- Transactional communication focuses on the what and the how, whilst transformational communication focuses on the why and meaning.

- There is a role for talking to your team, but it is equally important to listen to them. Ultimately, however, your role is to establish a culture where team members communicate amongst themselves spontaneously and effectively.

- There are many styles of team meeting, ranging from a formal set-piece briefing to an informal cosy team chat. Decide what styles suit your project's needs best and plan them with care.

- Deal with conflict early to limit its escalation, and prepare well, particularly if you need to intervene formally.
- Transformational communication means appealing to the heart as well as to the head.

PART 2

Leading your project team at each stage of the project

The essential insight of Part 1 was this: commit to the basics, do them well, do them consistently, and follow through.

This applies equally to Part 2, where you will lead your team through each stage of your project. In *Brilliant Project Leader*, we will assume a simple model of the life cycle of a project, with four stages. It is illustrated below.

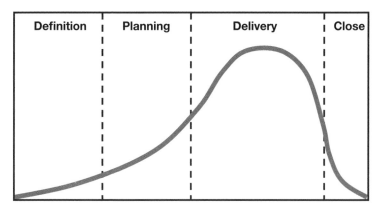

Project life cycle stages

Definition stage

The principal outcome from this stage is a clear definition of what your project is and is not. This stage is referred to by a number of alternative names, such as: outline planning, initiation, start-up, concept, briefing, or scoping.

Planning stage

The planning stage must answer three questions regarding your project:

1 **Why?**

A business case articulates the costs and benefits of your project and why it is therefore a sound proposition.

2 **What?**

A clear specification of all of the deliverables and the quality standards they must each meet.

3 **How?**

This is the plan itself, the tasks, the schedule, the resource and how they are deployed. It also contains your project controls; how you plan to stick to your plan, and what you will do if events force you away from it.

Delivery stage

In which you implement the plan and deliver the products (or deliverables) specified in your plan. Handing the last of these over to their new owner marks the end of the delivery stage and the start of the ...

Closure stage

Every project should be closed down in an orderly fashion.

Other stages

The joy of project leadership is its flexibility. Do feel free to add extra stages to your project if they will help you to lead your team, control your process or deliver greater accountability.

CHAPTER 6

Project definition stage

The two definitions of project management that you saw in the Introduction, from the US-based Project Management Institute and the UK-based Association for Project Management, differ in one fundamental respect. The PMI's definition focuses on the outputs, or deliverables, of a project: the physical services, products or results it produces. The UK definition focuses on the outcome of a project.

An outcome is the change that happens as a result of your project. So, for example, your output might be the construction of a new play area for local children. The outcomes once it is built might be happier, more physically active children and a social space for parents and carers. Or in a business context, your output might be a new computerised stock control and ordering system for your manufacturing plant. The desired outcomes could include smaller stock holdings, less working capital required, reduced financing costs and higher profit margins.

The difference between outputs – the physical products of your project – and outcomes – the changes that result – is important because project managers are most frequently charged with delivering outputs. Converting these into valuable outcomes for society, your organisation or your business is the business of other people such as service delivery or operational managers. But project leaders must interest themselves in the whole chain of value, and focus on the end outcome. It is a more strategic view than that of pure project management.

Project definition

The first and arguably most important step in creating a project is to define it. This means being very clear what your project is and what it is not, and creating a written definition statement that will guide every subsequent decision. There are three components to a project definition: your goal, objectives and scope.

Goal

Your goal articulates what the project will achieve. It answers the question:

'What do we want?'

Your leadership role is to ensure that the answer you get to this question really does serve your organisation. To test out your goal, ask the question 'For what purpose do we want this goal?' When you have the answer to that, look for other ways that you could serve this purpose. If the goal you stated for your project is the best possible way, then it is probably the right goal for your project: if not, then you need a different goal and a different project.

Challenging your project goal in this way will ensure that it links directly to the purpose and meaning that drive the organisation which is sponsoring your project. Not simply accepting a goal that is given to you but searching for the right project are an important facet of project leadership.

Wording your goal

Much of the language of project management is transactional: it needs to be clear, precise and technically accurate. But I recommend you try and lift the language that you use for your goal to a more transformational level and use words chosen to inspire. Your goal is the answer you will give me

the language of project management needs to be clear, precise and technically accurate when I ask 'What are you doing?' So, if you want to motivate me to join your project team, contribute funding or resources to your project, or simply support it vocally, your goal will help me decide. Think of how you word your goal as a part of 'marketing' your project, to create a 'brand' that has obvious value. Ideally, your goal will provide a compelling vision of 'What could be' to anybody interested in your project.

Naming your project

Not every project has a name, but many do. This becomes the most visible component of its 'brand identity' and a handy label to give your team an immediate sense of identity. Naming projects is a tricky business, with more people getting it wrong than right. The UK police forces keep a large list of names and whenever a new project or operation is launched, a name is randomly assigned. This keeps the name from giving away the nature of a potentially sensitive project or operation.

In most projects, however, it is best to have a name that clearly links to the project and its intended outcomes. Using your goal is one starting point for coming up with a name. Some project leaders see the responsibility to name the project as theirs alone, whilst others like to engage their team in a discussion or even a competition. However you want to approach it, here is some advice about what to do and what not to do.

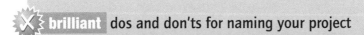

brilliant dos and don'ts for naming your project

Do

✔ Check very carefully for unintended alternative meanings.

✔ Choose a name that is a little out of the ordinary and therefore has fewer alternative associations.

✔ Pick something intriguing if you want people to ask about it.

▶

✔ Consider an emotive name that conjures up assumptions, feelings or emotions that are relevant.

✔ Use a randomly chosen name if your project is secret or confidential.

Don't

✘ Use meaningless, unpronounceable acronyms. People will forget what the name is and when asked what the acronym stands for, they will say, lamely, 'I don't know.' In particular avoid acronyms that accidentally spell out or suggest unwanted words, such as 'Social Housing Investment Trust'.

✘ Choose a name that is hard to pronounce in any language where the project might operate. If it is hard to pronounce, then people will avoid talking about it. Likewise, avoid hard-to-spell names.

✘ Pick a name that has unwanted alternative meanings either through double meanings or in a second language.

✘ Let your choice of name become divisive among your team, or alienate one or other of your stakeholder groups.

Maybe

? Use a word that has a similar meaning to or associations with the goal of your project.

? Pick a name from mythology, where there are a host of archetypes and associations. But don't be boring and stick solely to more familiar cultures like Ancient Greek or Roman. Take a look at http://www.godchecker.com.

? Literature, movies, music, drama and television provide a great source of names with culturally familiar associations. Be aware that if your project spans multiple cultures, this may be a problem.

? Use the name of someone famous – but not too famous – such as artists, composers, playwrights, architects, scientists or engineers. Avoid politicians or the law of unintended alternative meanings will certainly catch you out.

> **?** Geographical or geological features can make good names, such as rivers, mountains, minerals, volcanoes or seas; as can plant, animal or bird names, although many have been taken already as product names.
>
> **?** If all else fails, randomly flick through a dictionary or pick one of the *Apprentice* names in Chapter 4.

Objectives

Once you have a goal for your project, it is time to decide on its objectives. This will almost certainly mean consulting a variety of people and setting the criteria for its success, in terms of schedule, cost and quality. Objectives answer the question:

'How do we want it?'

That is, in achieving your goal, what standards must it meet, what deadline must it deliver to and how much should it cost? Objectives should be quantifiable statements than can subsequently be used as a standard to evaluate your project performance against.

SMART objectives

In drafting objectives, unlike goals, the precision of your language is far more important than its ability to inspire. Keep in mind the ideal that every objective you articulate is:

Specific	What precisely will the output or outcome be? In the planning stage, you will take this one step further to create detailed specifications.
Measurable	What numerical measures will you use to evaluate success, in terms of time, money, quantity, percentage improvements, or quality standards, for example?

Agreed	Objectives are useless if they are not agreed by the people with decision-making authority.
Realistic	You will want your objectives to be challenging so you can get the most out of the resources you deploy, but that needs to be tempered with realism. They must also be relevant – aligned with the mission and strategy of the sponsoring organisation.
Time-bound	For each objective – and some may be interim objectives, as well as final objectives – set a date for completion.

Scope

After goal and objectives comes scope. Scope determines the breadth and depth of your ambition for your project, and answers the question:

'How much of it do we want?'

You can think of scope in two different ways, although they relate directly to one another. In the UK, project managers tend to think more of the tasks that need to be done, so your project scope represents everything you need to do or take responsibility for. In the United States, project managers tend to think more of the products or deliverables that the project produces, so your project scope represents everything you need to create or commission.

Clearly, tasks lead to deliverables, so both ways of thinking are equivalent, but it is not a one-to-one relationship, so the two ways of thinking can give plans that look superficially different from one another. In the real world, many inexperienced project managers and people managing small, low-complexity projects will mix the two concepts of scope in their thinking and planning. It may seem heresy to formally trained project managers, but my experience is that there are many small projects where formality and precision are less important than the project team feeling comfortable with what they are doing, and this level of confusion is an acceptable compromise for quick and easy scoping that all of the team can understand easily.

Done

The reason for defining scope is to establish a baseline of what 'done' means: what is the complete set of tasks or deliverables that define your project as finished? Without this, there is a severe risk of one of the commonest causes of project failure: 'scope creep'.

Scope creep

Scope creep occurs when somebody within, or peripheral to, your project comes up to you or one of your team and says something like: 'While you are at it, could you just ...'. 'Could you just' are the three words project managers most fear, because they are rarely accompanied by the additional time, funds and resources that you need, to do the additional work without compromising your originally agreed scope. Unless you have a clearly defined scope – stating what your project will do and what it will not – you have no basis to reject scope creep.

> Unless you have a clearly defined scope you have no basis to reject scope creep

To further arm you to repel scope creep, get your statement of scope formally signed off by someone with the authority to say no when it is needed.

Note that this will not stop attempts at scope creep, nor should it stop important changes that arise from new conditions or new knowledge. But at least you have a clear baseline from which to assess the merits of changes. We'll look more at a process for dealing with scope and specification changes in Chapter 8.

Project leader skills for the definition stage

There are three particular leadership skills that you will need during the definition stage, as you navigate the turbulent waters around agreeing a final goal, objectives and scope for your project. Let's examine each in turn.

Managing upward

As project leader you will still be accountable to someone or, more likely, some people. These may be more senior managers in your organisation, non-executive directors, elected members or trustees, or clients or customers. Leadership means accepting their needs and requirements, while not becoming subservient to them and abandoning your own judgement and expertise.

> I don't want any yes men around me. I want everybody to tell me the truth even if it costs them their jobs.
>
> Samuel Goldwyn

Discuss mutual expectations

Start with what you each want from your involvement as project leader and then move on to understand their aims and how they see them fitting in with the organisation's wider mission and strategy. Use this to develop a goal and then move to objectives. Here, your first and most important question will establish where their priorities lie among time, cost and quality. They cannot prioritise all three, so you need to know the relative importance they attach to each. This will act as your compass, guiding you in every subsequent decision. If senior people or clients disagree over this fundamental matter, you may need to get them all into one meeting, to resolve the issues among themselves.

Timing

Good upward management means using the time of senior people with care, or they will quickly learn to avoid you. Schedule meetings when you can, and give clear guidance on when you need a decision. Above all, try and avoid surprises by giving advance notice of what you need to discuss, so they can feel prepared, rather than ambushed.

brilliant tip

At the start of a meeting with a senior person, make your first question this:

'How much time do we have?'

Get to know them

You may think that, in the light of time pressures, you need to avoid taking extra time for rapport building. This will be true for certain people – it is their style to be abrupt and straight to the point. However, with most, thirty seconds of pleasantries is an important opener to the substantive conversation.

Rapport also helps you learn about their style, preferences and personal strengths. All of this information will help you adapt your approach to theirs, and get the best from your exchanges.

Structure your argument

There is a simple four-step process, FARB, for structuring an effective argument.

Facts	Start with the facts and evidence, summarised concisely.
Analysis	Then give your analysis of what the evidence means.
Recommendations	State your recommendation clearly.

Benefits   Spell out the benefits of adopting your
                        recommendation.

Note that with controlling individuals, you may want to leave
out the benefits – and possibly even your recommendations.
Let the facts and analysis speak for themselves and allow the
decision maker to come to their own conclusion. If they have
a controlling personality, then they don't like to be told what
to do. If they do adopt your recommendation and then it goes
wrong, they will see you as a scapegoat, rather than take responsibility for their decision.

Only fight the battles you need to fight
When you have a leadership role, it is tempting to think you
must always be right. In truth, it is often far more important
to select when you need to be right and when to back down
because the difference is unimportant. Know when to concede
entirely, when to compromise and when to fight hard for your
point of view to prevail.

Stakeholder management

Agreeing the scope of your project is often the hardest part of
leading it. There will be many people with opinions, and many
of these opinions will conflict with one another. You will need to
conduct a negotiation among all of these people, whom we term
stakeholders.

 brilliant definition

Stakeholder
A stakeholder is anyone (or any organisation) that has an interest
in your project.

We'll tackle negotiation in a moment, but it is worth spelling out,
simply, a four-step process for managing your stakeholders. This
will start at the definition stage of your project, and continue
through to the final close-down.

Four-step process

Stakeholder management follows a simple four-step process.

Step 1: Identify your stakeholders

Work with team members to list anyone or any group of people who have an interest in your project, its outcome or its progress, or who is in any way affected by how it happens or what it produces.

Step 2: Analyse your stakeholders

The more you can know about your stakeholders, the better you will be able to manage them, so consider their interests, their likely perceptions of the project, their levels of influence and power, who they know, what they stand to lose or gain, their needs and expectations, and what you want or need from them.

Step 3: Plan your campaign

How will you tackle each stakeholder? Will you seek to persuade them, inform them, engage them and use their influence, marginalise them, empower them, or simply keep an eye on them? What messages will you need to communicate to them, and how and when?

Step 4: Take action

Carry out your plan. Constantly monitor your progress and review your plan in the light of what you are learning.

Negotiation

Developing an agreed scope that ensures that all of the 'musts' are included and that you can balance all of the 'wants' with the resources available is a big negotiating task. The more stakeholders want, the more resources you will need to secure. The more your resources are constrained, the more you will need to say no. As P. T. Barnum could have said, 'You can please some of the people all of the time and all of the people some of the time, but you can't please all of the people all of the time.' Part of your role is therefore to know who you need to please and who you can afford to disappoint.

Just say no

When negotiating scope, the safest approach is to determine the minimum possible scope that delivers to the core, mandatory capabilities needed to achieve the project's goal and objectives and then practise using one word in a variety of creative (but explicit) ways: no. Assume that any additional requirement must be proven before you will add it to your project scope, because if you start by saying yes, you *will* have to go back to some stakeholders later on and disappoint them with the news that their cherished capabilities have been cut from the project. It is far better to under-promise and be able later to over-deliver, than to promise the world and deliver a car park.

> It is better to under-promise and be able to over-deliver

Facilitating role

All project managers and most project leaders have purely facilitating roles during these negotiations. What therefore distinguishes these roles are the way you conduct the process and lead it by setting agendas and winning consensus, rather than feel buffeted by changing moods and priorities.

As a facilitator, what will often determine your success is the quality of the questions that you ask participants in the process. Prepare well for meetings and search for those questions that will unlock deep understanding and a recognition of the true purpose and meaning behind your project. Find ways to separate self-interest from the common good, and avoid trying to manipulate the situation with leading questions; this can only lead to weak commitment from stakeholders that can later unravel.

Influencing and persuading

Brilliant Influence is a good companion to this part of *Brilliant Project Leader*. It not only covers the basics of negotiation but also contains a wealth of insights into human psychology.

⤴ brilliant tactics for influencing and persuading

1   Start with small talk: brilliant project leaders build great rapport.

2   Dress well, adopt a confident posture and a warm smile: brilliant project leaders know how to make a strong personal impact.

3   Establish your credibility: brilliant project leaders have the authority to drive a consensus.

4   Look for overlapping outcomes among stakeholders: brilliant project leaders know that win-win comes from answering 'What's in it for me?'

5   Find the common ground on which you can both agree: brilliant project leaders prefer to say yes.

6   Separate dissenters and put them with committed supporters: brilliant project leaders know that peer pressure is a powerful persuader and that two or more dissenters can reinforce each other's views.

7   Listen more than you speak: brilliant project leaders seek to gather and use others' ideas.

8   Respect what you hear: brilliant project leaders listen hardest when the message is most challenging.

9   Move the body, move the mind: brilliant project leaders know when to get up and walk around with the people they are negotiating with.

10 Set a deadline: brilliant project leaders use time pressure effectively to focus minds and get a result.

11 Document each agreement you get, and publish it: brilliant project leaders know that once we have made a public commitment, it is hard to reverse our position.

12 Always give a reason for the other person to change their mind:

brilliant project leaders always give a new morsel of information. Without it they are asking someone to change their mind. With it, they are asking for a new decision.

Project kick-off

Early on, you need to engage people in your project by convincing them that it really matters and that they should commit to their role in making it happen. A project kick-off workshop is a good way to do this.

Hierarchy of meaning

Start by placing your project in context, within the hierarchy of meaning we discussed in Chapter 3. Spell out your project's goal and purpose, what the outcomes will be and what impact it will have on customers, clients, colleagues, service users or the public. Then articulate the objectives and scope of the project, ending with the broad areas of work, and who you will be asking to contribute to each.

Moving towards a plan

Many kick-off meetings can harness the energy this first part generates, to start work on planning aspects of the project. It is a great way to start building teamwork among unfamiliar colleagues too. Examples of good activities to include here are:

- Stakeholder identification and assessment
- Listing tasks or deliverables for a work breakdown structure (see Chapter 7)
- Generating a list of possible risks to the project
- Identifying assumptions that need to be tested, or uncertainties that need to be resolved
- Reviewing other known activities, initiatives and projects to

see where there are interdependencies, constraints or other linkages

● Inventorying the skills, experience and knowledge of team members.

Leadership and governance

Leadership and good governance go together. In the context of a project, this means establishing effective arrangements for two principal governance roles: oversight and decision making. There are as many different structures to achieve this as there are projects, but a few principles are worth noting.

Project board

Project boards are too often filled with 'the great and the good' and consequently act as little more than a talking shop and the opportunity to claim a part of any future success. So use your influence to help design your project board's membership and procedures to serve your project's governance needs well.

Create a balance of roles so that users and suppliers are represented, and there is expertise present to help the board arbitrate between them. The ideal size for your board is five, six or seven members. Any more members and it will struggle to stay on agenda and there will be too many ways for members to hide from their responsibilities. Too few members and you will not get the balance of knowledge and experience for the discussion you need for good oversight and decision making.

Project sponsor

In most organisations, the project board has ultimate accountability for the project and will take responsibility for all the most fundamental decisions. The project sponsor is a senior executive, who usually serves on the board, whose primary role is to promote the project both internally and externally (sponsor it) and act as a kind of line manager to the project manager/ leader. In this latter role, they will adopt some of the board's responsibilities for oversight and decision making, as well as advising and supporting roles.

In some organisations – including the UK public sector, where the project sponsor is called the Senior Responsible Owner or SRO – one individual is named as responsible for ensuring the project meets its goal and objectives, and delivers the planned benefits. They will be held accountable.

Steering group

The term 'steering group' is sometimes used interchangeably with project board, but is better reserved for a group of advisors or stakeholders that will have input into project decision making via a single person who also sits on the project board. This is a way of increasing the number of people who can make a structured contribution to project decisions, without letting the project board grow to an unwieldy size.

Project assurance

Larger, more complex, more strategically vital projects will have a layer of oversight from outside the project structure, giving it a greater measure of objectivity. This can come from within or even outside the project's sponsoring organisation and would typically be conducted by experienced project professionals.

Effective, accountable decision making

In a project environment, there are three conditions for a 'sound decision'. None of them is that the decision has to be right, however. Projects are uncertain ventures and you will make mistakes; it is part of the process. But if you respect these three requirements, you will limit the number and scale of the mistakes you make.

1 **Evidence based**
   Project decisions need to be based on the best available
   evidence.

2 **Sound process**
   Put in place a robust process for making a decision, which
   must involve a thorough analysis of the evidence and an
   opportunity to challenge and critique both the evidence and
   the analysis.

3 **The right people**
   Decisions must be made by people with the right level of
   authority, the right skills and knowledge, and sufficient time
   to consider their decision.

 The alternative to evidence-based decision making is
decision-based evidence-making.

Adapted from an aphorism I first heard from Tony Quigley

The future evolution of your team

Most project teams first come together during or towards the
end of the definition stage, although additional members may be
introduced during the planning and at the start of the delivery
stages too.

So now is a good time to examine how a team evolves from a
group of strangers to the high-performing team that any project
leader will dream of. A coherent model of group formation
and team evolution was first developed in the 1960s by Bruce
Tuckman. Teams don't always follow this pattern precisely, but
often follow a very similar trajectory.

Forming

When a group comes together for the first time, they are uncertain of their roles and eager to please. They quickly start to size

each other up and form alliances, but would really like to know what is expected of them.

Your leadership role is therefore to set straightforward tasks where group members can work together without needing strong bonds of trust – which is why the activities identified above, like listing stakeholders, are so helpful. Don't compete with your team, but show yourself to be a calm, steady presence, spending time listening and building your relationships.

> Don't compete with your team, but show yourself to be a calm, steady presence

Storming

After a while, people start to get to know one another and inhibitions start to fall. At the same time, they naturally start to become concerned with their individual roles in the team and where they sit in the pecking order. They will start to compete with one another and to challenge your leadership – particularly the most dominant members of the group. This is a high-energy stage, and gradually, as the team aligns, you can turn that energy into creativity.

At this stage you must assert your leadership and ensure that you set out a clear agenda for the team. Reassure and instil confidence in the less assertive group members and give clear signals to the others that you are in charge. Allow the team time to argue and debate, as these are a natural part of the process, and start to allocate specific roles fairly and on merit, based on expertise, experience, capability and potential.

Norming

Eventually the team will settle down and start to get on with its work. Now people will find that focusing on their own work is an escape from the psychologically intense storming phase. So this is a productive stage where the team starts to work out its modes or 'norms' of working together. This is where any team charter will start to bed down.

You role as leader is primarily to make the links between team members so that they can go beyond working in isolation or small groups. If you sense Abbie needs some advice, ask Diego to help her out. If you see Charumati with some time to spare, ask her to lend a hand to Boris, who seems to be overstretched. This way you are starting to build powerful working relationships that span your team.

Performing

Once your team reaches the performing stage, everyone is comfortable working together, making the team a happy and productive environment for all. People share responsibilities, consult one another and enjoy each other's company. An outsider looking in would be hard-pressed to spot who is in charge: different people will step forward at different times to take the lead when the team is focused on something they are passionate about or expert in. Then they will step back and let someone else take the lead as the team's agenda moves on.

As leader, you need to exert a very light touch. The team no longer needs much direction and neither do they need you to support their working relationships. Your primary role now is to maintain the environment in which the team can thrive, protecting them from intrusions, like a lightning rod, and feeding them information and securing the resources they need to do their job. From time to time, you may need to intervene, with some advice here, diffusing some tension there and making leadership decisions.

But there is more ...

'Performing' is not quite the end of the story. But you will have to wait until Chapters 8 and 9 to find out what happens next.

Brilliant definition

Creating a brilliant project at this stage requires a worthwhile goal, which you can express in an inspiring way. Focus on how your project will help people or do something that really matters. Or maybe it is exciting for its own sake: innovative, radical or beautiful.

The more you can do to involve your team in shaping your project, the more they will feel a sense of ownership and commitment to it. Encourage them to be innovative and radical and to challenge boundaries and guidelines, whilst confidently guarding the process from unnecessary risk or inappropriate excesses. By their making it their project, it becomes brilliant.

 brilliant recap

- The project definition consists of a goal, objectives and a statement of the project scope. Write SMART objectives and defend from scope creep.
- A brilliant project leader must master the skills of managing upward, stakeholder management and negotiation.
- A project kick-off meeting can inform and motivate your team and start work on planning your project too.
- Good governance is a vital part of leadership, and requires two things: oversight and effective, accountable decision making.
- Teams evolve through distinct stages, and your leadership role changes as your team evolves.

CHAPTER 7

Project planning stage

During the planning stage, you and your team must create definitive answers to three questions:

What? Full and detailed specifications of each of your project's deliverables

Why? A business case or investment appraisal that demonstrates why your sponsoring organisation should commit the funds and resources to delivering your project

How? Your project plan will show how you intend to deliver your project, and your project controls will demonstrate how you will manage your plan day to day.

Planning and scheduling your project are crucial project management disciplines. In this chapter, we will focus on the leadership elements of project planning. Some might argue that planning is not a leadership matter at all, but General (later President) Dwight D. Eisenhower was a military and civil leader who made the point very clearly.

 In preparing for battle I have always found that plans are useless, but planning is indispensable.

Dwight D. Eisenhower

You may or may not be able to stick to your plan, but by going through the process, you will have a far better understanding of what is happening. Your project controls will help you stay on plan and, if you need to make changes, will help you to stay in control.

The elements of a project plan

As with chemicals and their elements, project plans have components from which everything can be built. The most important of these are products, activities, sequence, time, resources and risks. These are presented in the order that you would most often consider them in a formal planning process.

Products

When we discussed project scope in the previous chapter, we saw how it can be considered as 'all the things that need to be done' or 'all the things that need to be produced'. Whichever way you view your scope, formal planning starts with the products, or things. These are the answer to the 'What?' question, and from this you need your team to produce a full list of deliverables that the project will produce.

Your leadership role is to ensure that there is a final reconciliation between this list, the specifications for each item, the project's goal and objectives, and the needs and expectations of your primary stakeholders. If these do not reconcile, then you are storing up a significant problem for yourself.

Activities

Each product needs to be produced and the production of each needs to be coordinated. This leads to all of the project's activities, or tasks. Project managers construct this complete task list into a structured hierarchy, known in the UK as a work breakdown structure (WBS). Note that in the United States, the term

WBS refers to a structured hierarchy of the products, rather than tasks (in the UK, we call this a product breakdown structure). The distinction is significant because the product hierarchy will often follow an inevitable logic dictated by the civil, mechanical, electronic or software engineering or social, political or organisational relationships between the products. There is a lot more freedom in how you can structure a hierarchy of activities.

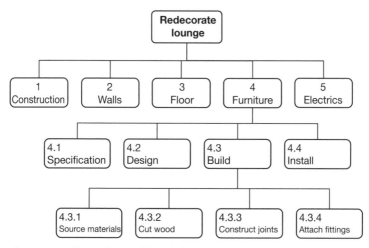

Figure 7.1 Illustrative work breakdown structure

In Figure 7.1, we have followed one route through the WBS, for illustrative purposes. Because of the complexity of drawing out a full WBS, we usually prefer to number the items, as illustrated, and present it in a tabular form.

Your leadership role is to decide which approach will best serve your project: task or product orientation? Then you need to consider how to structure your WBS to give most clarity to your plan. In a task-oriented WBS, you can, for example, structure activities according to: organisational

> decide which approach will best serve your project: task or product orientation

convenience, personnel structures, function, trades or expert areas, geographical considerations, schedule phases or engineering constraints.

Sequence

Once you know what you need to do, the next planning step is to examine the logical sequence of your activities. This creates what is generically known as a 'network chart'. This links together your project activities to highlight the dependencies between the completion of one activity and the start of the next (a finish-to-start dependency). Other dependencies are also possible, such as finish-to-finish or start-to-start, but are less common. There are two principal standard methodologies for creating network charts, called PERT (programme evaluation and review technique) and critical path analysis (CPA). The latter gives us our widely used but less widely understood term, 'critical path'. We will define this when we have looked at the time component of your plan, in a moment.

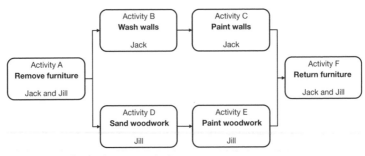

Figure 7.2 Illustrative network chart

A good project manager will spend a lot of time examining and testing out the logic of their project network. As a project leader, you can harness the different skills and perspectives of your team to help with this. A carefully channelled sense of competition can often create deep analysis and objectivity, and many project leaders use the idea of 'red team reviews' to split planning teams in two and ask one group to critique the work of the other. This may seem to add a lot of extra overhead to the planning process but, for a large and complex project, this is time well invested, if it discovers flaws in your planning ahead of commissioning contractors and materials, and starting work on delivery.

Time

Now you can start to schedule activities to bring time into your plan – making what is sometimes referred to as a programme, although the word has other uses too. Strictly, a network only becomes a PERT chart or CPA once time is incorporated. Now you can calculate how long your project will take. The critical path is the longest route through the network. Consequently, it tells you how long your project will take. It is 'critical' in the sense that if any activity on your critical path is delayed, then the whole project will be delayed.

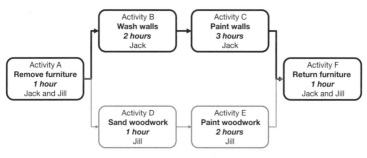

Figure 7.3 Illustrative critical path

Therefore, to reduce the risk of delay, you need to apply contingency to activities on the critical path, to break the critical path. Negotiating extra time is very much a leadership role. If you put in too much contingency, you are open to challenge that your planning is wasteful, yet if you put in too little, your risk of schedule slippage is high. Project leaders are often called upon to defend their decisions to apply contingency, and will be familiar with statements like this:

'I could schedule an earlier completion date, but I would not be confident that we could achieve this. The extra time scheduled for contingencies allows me to offer you a very high confidence of delivery to this schedule.'

We looked in the last chapter at managing upward and this is one of the commonest examples; whether as a conversation with senior managers, directors or non-executives in your own organisation, or with a customer or client.

Milestones

Another tool that project managers use for planning and controlling the time element of a project are 'milestones': fixed points in the project when something happens – most often, the completion of something significant. Project managers use milestones to give an outline structure to their plan, and as a tool to support monitoring and controlling progress. Project leaders also use milestones to mark points in their project where they will be able to celebrate success, and so motivate their team.

Gantt charts

Gantt charts – sometimes called bar charts – are a widely used way to visualise project plans, combining activities with schedule in a simple graphic. Most people like them, some find them

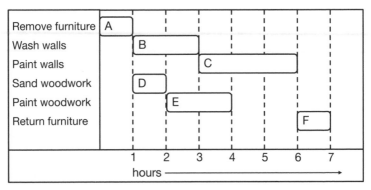

Figure 7.4 Illustrative Gantt chart

confusing, and a few hate them. They are a project planning and monitoring tool for project managers.

In your project leader role, the important consideration is how you will communicate your plan and, subsequently, your progress. Visual tools like the Gantt chart will often be the best way; however, you should make no assumptions: speak with your stakeholders and find out what information they want and need, and how they would best like it presented. Choosing your presentation tools is a different matter from selecting planning and monitoring tools, and is very much a leadership role.

Resources

There are four types of resource to consider on a typical project: people, money, assets and materials. Each task needs someone or some people to do it, has a cost, and potentially uses assets and materials in its completion. Now your planning must add these to your plan, and the easiest starting place is your work breakdown structure. When you add a cost to each item in your WBS, you get a cost breakdown structure, or CBS. This is the easiest way to develop a project budget.

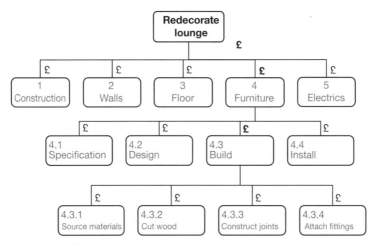

Figure 7.5 Illustrative cost breakdown structure

You can also allocate people to each element of your WBS, to get an organisational breakdown structure (OBS). When you allocate leadership of a cluster of activities to one person, as illustrated in Figure 7.6, the group of activities is called a work stream, and the leader is either the work-stream leader or work-stream manager.

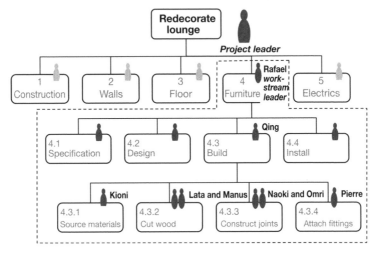

Figure 7.6 Illustrative organisational breakdown structure

Deploying your team and making decisions about management and leadership structures are an important way to demonstrate trust and offer development opportunities. In a highly technical project, most project leaders will appoint their work-stream leaders early on and ask them to plan and resource their own work streams. Your role as project leader becomes one of evaluating and testing out their assumptions and plans, and ensuring that their collective planning is properly coordinated.

Risks

We have identified risks as the final one of the most important elements of planning. Experienced project managers know that risks are part of a cluster of planning considerations: DCARI, which stands for: dependencies, constraints, assumptions, risks and issues. Risk management, however, is a major activity on all projects.

The leadership element of risk management concentrates on two aspects: ensuring that 'upside risks' are equally planned for, and determining the right level of risk for your project: your 'risk appetite'.

Upside risks

A risk is an uncertainty that can affect outcomes. It can have a positive (opportunity) or a negative (threat) effect. Most project risk management focuses on the threats that risks can pose, but if you don't try to anticipate and plan for opportunities, one may come and then

> try to anticipate and plan for opportunities, one may pass you by, simply because you failed to recognise it

pass you by, simply because you failed to recognise it or, recognising it, you might not know how to capitalise on it.

Make sure that your team applies all of its risk management processes to identifying, understanding and planning for opportunities.

Risk appetite

How much risk should your project take? Anyone tempted to answer 'none' is being naive, foolish or disingenuous. Risk is an inevitable part of life and certainly a part of projects, where novelty and therefore uncertainty are defining characteristics. So the perfectly reasonable question to ask is: 'How much risk should your project take?'

As project leader, you must wrestle with your project's and your organisation's appetite for risk. We saw this, in one specific guise, when we looked at time, above. You could promise earlier delivery, offering the consequent advantages to your sponsor or your client, but at a greater risk that plans will need to change at the last minute. There are a number of considerations to take into account when considering how much risk to incur, or how cautious to be:

● The prevailing culture of your organisation (and that of your customer or client)

● The personalities of key stakeholders

● The ability to absorb the consequences of risk without damage

● The availability of resources to mitigate risks

● The project's level of innovation and novelty.

We will discuss this last point in more detail, later in this chapter.

Plan how to use your team

The organisational breakdown structure is one way to plan your resource deployment. There are two other tools which are very useful in helping a project leader to coordinate their team.

Allocating roles: the linear responsibility chart (LRC)

The linear responsibility chart is one of the simplest and best project planning tools and is a great way to communicate simply and powerfully what each person is committed to doing, so that your whole team can see what they and their colleagues are working on and with whom they need to collaborate on each task.

In Figure 7.7, you can see that the team members are listed across the top of the chart, and down the side are listed the tasks. You could equally list work streams, if you wanted a higher-level view of your project, or even a list of projects, if you were leading a number of projects at the same time.

In the intersections, you can use words, letters, or symbols to illustrate the roles that each person is fulfilling. In the United

States, this is often called a RACI chart, after four common roles: responsible, authority, consulted and informed. The illustration shows four different roles, so choose a set of roles that is helpful to you and your team.

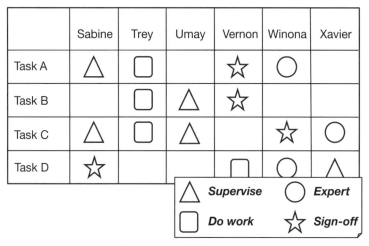

	Sabine	Trey	Umay	Vernon	Winona	Xavier
Task A	△	☐		☆	○	
Task B		☐	△	☆		
Task C	△	☐	△		☆	○
Task D	☆			☐	○	△

△ Supervise   ○ Expert
☐ Do work   ☆ Sign-off

Figure 7.7 Illustrative linear responsibility chart

This is a great communication tool. It lets you and your team see the balance of workload easily. You can correct imbalances and the team can see that workloads are equitable, and you can also see that each task has the right mix of resources.

Securing commitment: the work package definition (WPD)

Often, you will find a project team member makes a promise to do a piece of work and then fails to deliver. How can you increase your chances of securing compliance? The answer is a piece of psychology I call 'the Jiminy Cricket effect' after Pinocchio's friend, who acts as his conscience.

If I ask you to do something and leave it at that, you may or may not do it, according to a number of factors. If, however, I ask you and wait for an answer, there are only two possibilities: either yes or no. I will interpret an equivocal answer like 'maybe' or a hesitant 'yes' as a 'no'. If the answer is yes, then you have awakened Jiminy Cricket. He is now alert and, if you are about to break your promise, he will go on at you to keep it. This kind of brain ache is what neuroscientists call 'cognitive dissonance' – the mismatch between your feeling that you are an honest person of integrity and the concern that you are about to break your word.

Notice two things: first, this won't work if you are content to be seen as someone who breaks their word and, second, the more publicly you make your commitment, the greater the pressure that Jiminy Cricket will put on you to honour it. Getting a yes in a team meeting is far more powerful than one to one: now Jiminy is protecting you from lying to a whole bunch of valued colleagues.

But what if you said no, or something that amounted to the same thing? Well, at least I know straight away and can handle the situation without falsely believing that, two weeks later, the job will be done. I could ask someone else; I could apply some pressure; or I could ask for the reason, or what would stop you, or what would need to change for you to say yes. For example:

'I understand you can't commit to this now, and thank you for being so frank with me. What could I do to help you, which would allow you to say yes?'

'If you cannot do this for us, what is getting in the way? Is there anything we can do to make it possible?'

⤢ brilliant tool

The work package definition is a way to formalise this commitment. It consists of a written statement of the work I am assigning to you, with a chance for you to sign, to accept it. It's like putting Jiminy Cricket on amphetamine! Here is a simple template you can adapt.

Work Package Definition		Version No. ....

WP Title: .... Date: ....

Output required	*List of required deliverables and their key attributes*
Completion criteria	*Required quality controls and approvals*
Activity description	*Functional description of work required, broken down to an appropriate level of detail*
Inputs/dependencies and other resources	*References to known inputs/dependencies, standards and other constraints, available tools and resources*
Estimated effort	*Effort allocated for WBS activities – indicate units used*
Planned timescale	*Date planned for work package completion, and any other milestone dates*

Assigned by:	*Signature*	Date: ....
Accepted by:	*Signature*	Date: ....

You can use a WPD whenever you have less confidence in compliance than you would like. They are also used when an audit trail is necessary, such as in cases of safety-related activities, or to document contractual commitments.

Risk taking and innovation

Calculated risk taking is a leadership tool that can get more from less. By 'calculated', I mean that you will have evaluated not just the potential benefits, but everything that could go wrong and its potential impacts, and estimated the relative likelihoods of different scenarios playing out. This is where a 'sound decision', as described in Chapter 6 is crucial.

The criteria for 'good' risk taking

Innovation demands a measure of risk taking, but how can you get that balance right? Here are four criteria to consider.

1 **Information**
   Do you have good data and strong analytical tools to understand the risk?

2 **Confidence**
   Team self-confidence comes from the support and trust of the leader and the hierarchy, and a climate of trust among colleagues.

3 **Listening**
   Does everybody listen to and respect all opinions, no matter how contrary or concerned? Good facilitation and a clear shared understanding of the goal, objectives and scope of your project are vital.

4 **Diversity**
   Different perspectives, knowledge, experiences, styles and skills make a fair analysis of risks and benefits more likely.

Your team's role: group-think versus team-think

When a coherent group debates a tricky issue, they can often settle on a position that leaves some members feeling, privately, uncomfortable. However, rather than upset colleagues, they remain silent, thinking their concerns are unshared or unreasonable. There is no critical challenge because team harmony is put above right action, and because the information everyone discusses is the information everyone knows. New ideas or evidence are suppressed. This is called *'group-think'* and was first named and described in the 1970s by Irving Janis.

Risky shift

It gets worse, because if you can persuade me and our group to accept your position, you become emboldened, and the group's position can shift further in a process called 'risky shift'. Groups can tend to endorse more extreme positions (either higher risk or lower risk) than any individual would have accepted, leading to catastrophic errors.

Countering group-think

Countering group-think and moving to effective team decisions and risk taking means moving to what I call 'team-think'. The characteristics of team-think are:

1 **Diversity**

Creating a diverse team and encouraging different opinions.

Tip: If you have a team that has worked together for a long time, introduce a non-expert who will see things differently.

2 **Independence**

Each person thinks for themselves and the process ensures that everyone will be heard and listened to.

Tip: Brief people beforehand and ask them to come to the meeting with ideas.

3 **Challenge**

The process encourages people to challenge data, interpretations and conclusions robustly, and ensures that all opinions are evaluated.

Tip: Either assign someone to challenge the rest of the team, or take periodic time-outs when you ask the whole team to review what it has done critically, by looking for gaps in reasoning or risks arising from the emerging consensus.

4 **Decentralisation**

Everyone has independent access to all of the data, to avoid bias creeping into its gathering and selection.

Tip: Circulate raw data, and identify the sources of the data. Allow people to interrogate those sources for themselves.

5 **Equality**

Leaders and experts who express an opinion early on will usually frame the whole discussion. Ensure that discussions start with facts and that leaders do not contribute opinions early on for fear of biasing debate.

Tip: Encourage the quieter, more reticent people to contribute. Consider using anonymous contribution methods to gather ideas and encourage contrarian viewpoints.

6 **Objectivity**

One way to counter group-think is to invite an independent third party to join a discussion, bringing fresh ideas and an outsider's perspective.

Tip: Ask an objective colleague to sit in and challenge what is being said.

Planning to learn: pilots, prototypes and tests

One valuable approach to balancing risk and innovation is to plan opportunities into your project, to learn and refine your plans and risk profile. In particular, design tests to 'break' your ideas, rather than prove them. It is not possible to prove that something will work under all conditions, so a demonstration that it does work tells you little. To gain confidence, you have to push it to and even beyond the outer limits of

design tests to 'break' your ideas, rather than prove them

its design capabilities. If it then fails to break, your confidence can increase.

Pilots and prototypes are 'no-lose' initiatives. If they succeed and the test objects do not go wrong, they are hugely motivating to your supporters and put a real dent in the arguments of your critics. If, on the other hand, your pilot or prototype fails, that's good news: you have a chance to learn and have avoided a costly failure in a real situation.

In designing a test, a pilot or a prototype, as always begin with the outcome you want. Ask:

- What do we want to learn?
- What failure modes do we want to explore?
- What do stakeholders need to test, experience, evaluate?
- What politically do we want to achieve?
- Who do we want to involve?

Leading a virtual team

Increasingly, project leaders have to lead teams that are not all in the same place, at the same time. These are known as virtual teams and, on some projects, they can quite literally span the globe, with members in East Asia, Europe, Africa, South America and the Pacific North West. To communicate, team members rely on a variety of modern technology, including tele- and video-conferencing, instant messaging, virtual communities and discussion boards and internet tools like Skype, SkyDrive, Campfire and Connect. They can operate 24 hours a day and bring rich rewards in terms of diversity and novelty, but they also present challenges.

We are still in a learning phase with virtual teams and any books or advice must still be considered provisional. The main challenge is the unfamiliarity for many project leaders. Whilst some of the familiar 'rules' of team leadership still apply, others do not, but one thing will always remain true: virtual teams are still about real people. Don't let the distance or technology seduce you into forgetting the basic fact that relationships still matter.

Another significant challenge is culture. Whilst a small number of people in the same place can readily adopt a common working culture, the more dispersed your team, the harder this is to create – especially as each team member will bring more diverse cultural norms as a starting point. What you can achieve is to create some norms of how the team will work together at the touch-points where people in different parts of the team come together. Things to think about are:

● How to ensure common understandings – particularly over social, emotional and cultural matters, rather than objective facts like technical specifications or sales data. Even so, these too can present risks – one Mars lander crashed when the European Space Agency and NASA failed to be explicit about which measurements were in imperial units and which in metric.

● What courtesies and formalities are necessary to ensure that everybody feels comfortable? These can include greetings, respecting of status and hierarchy, how feedback is given and received, and use of language. Indeed, which language or languages the team uses can be a matter of concern.

● The style of leadership you adopt, and how you communicate ideas and instructions.

● The use of culturally variant symbols. For example, the Japanese have a different range of colour hues that they describe as 'green' compared with Western Europeans and North Americans, and the Chinese have a different set of culturally determined mental associations with red from those in Western Europe and North America.

- How you are going to deal with thorny matters like conflict and reprimands – especially when your virtual team's work patterns can delay you in tackling something that is best dealt with immediately.

- The frequency with which the team 'meets' and, indeed how, whether and when to get the team together physically.

Brilliant planning

Three elements of brilliant planning go into making a brilliant project. First, whatever you plan, make sure you under-promise against what you believe is possible. This gives you the opportunity to over-deliver, which can leave your team, your client, your bosses and all of your stakeholders really delighted.

Second, make liberal use of pilots, prototypes and planned testing. The opportunity for team members and stakeholders to get their hands on something real can create a palpable buzz around your project as well as the chance to learn more.

Finally, success breeds success; nothing is more motivating for your supporters, nor more effective in countering critics. Success builds momentum and instils confidence that leads to better performance and more success. Plan in milestones that will allow you to mark and celebrate project successes at regular and frequent intervals.

Note: you can download a range of project planning templates from www.brilliantprojectleader.co.uk.

 **brilliant** recap

- At the planning stage, answer the questions what, why and how.

- Your plan needs to accommodate the products your project will create, the activities it needs to undertake, the sequence and timing of those activities, the resources you will need, and the risks that will arise.

- For project leaders, their team is their most valued resource. Use a linear responsibility chart to communicate responsibilities and, if you need to, use commitment and the 'Jiminy Cricket effect' to drive consistent behaviour.

- Understand the nature of risk taking and how to make sound decisions. Avoid the threats of group-think and risky shift.

- Virtual teams are dispersed in time and space, so leading them takes special consideration.

CHAPTER 8

Project
delivery stage

The delivery stage of your project is where you get to relax. Find a comfy chair, get a cup of fresh coffee and put your feet up. You've done the hard work of defining your project, creating detailed plans and briefing your team. Now it is time for them to do the work.

If only. Yet there is some truth in this caricature. Your job *is* to let your team do their work, with minimum interference, but this does not mean you have no role to play: you must support them, coordinate them, monitor team and project performance, keep your stakeholders happy, and hand over completed project deliverables to your client, your boss, or the operational managers who will take responsibility for them.

Monitor and control

'Management by walking about' goes in and out of fashion as a concept, but the underlying principle of staying close to your team is sound. If you make it a central part of what you do at all times, rather than when you feel there are problems, you will avoid the suspicion that you simply want to check up on people. Use it to gauge mood, provide ideas, share good news and hear about people's successes.

Hold your more formal monitoring conversations with workstream leaders and let them lead their work streams and monitor their teams formally themselves.

 **example**

On one project, I would meet first thing in the morning with all of my work-stream leaders for them to share status and concerns, and coordinate their work. Then, during the day, I would meet each one individually to discuss progress against plan, review outputs and help with any issues that had arisen. Towards the end of each day, I'd wander around the whole project team, chatting with individual members and hearing how they were getting on. This was partly about listening to individuals and partly about taking the temperature of the team. Any concerns I had would then get discussed with work-stream leaders, either as a group or individually.

The monitor and control loop

The formal monitoring process can best be represented as a 'control cycle', or 'monitor and control loop'. This is illustrated below.

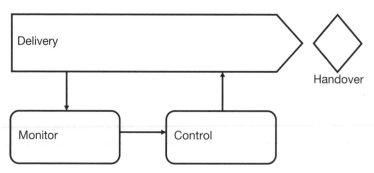

Monitor and control loop

Your primary project management role in the delivery stage is to know what is going on in all aspects of your project. As issues emerge and events put pressure on your plan, you will need to make decisions that will help you control your project's progress. The skill is in going around the control cycle rapidly enough to ensure you catch issues and problems when they are small, so that your interventions can be simple and will easily resolve the matter and bring you back on plan.

Your leadership challenge is to know how much of the control to leave with work-stream leaders and individuals, and how much to exert yourself. If you or your team do not spot problems and deal with them quickly enough, they can soon grow and your interventions will need to be bigger and costlier, and will bear higher risk.

Another judgement that you will need to make constantly is the depth of your monitoring: whether to see your project through a wide-angle panoramic lens or a close-up macro lens. As a good project leader, you must be able to change your focus rapidly: constantly aware of the broad picture, but able to zoom in on any detail and give it your full attention at any time. It is not good enough to 'stay strategic' and refuse to engage in the detail – which may well bore you – when the situation demands it. Equally, if you get too caught up in the detail and cannot draw yourself back for an overview of the whole project, you will not be able to balance your attention appropriately across all its components.

> change your focus rapidly: be constantly aware of the broad picture, but able to zoom in on any detail

Reporting

You also have a responsibility to report progress to your client, your boss, your sponsor and your project board. This serves two purposes: communication and governance.

Communicating status is important for accountability, but it also allows others to act in an informed manner, to support you and your team. Team members also need a comprehensive picture of the project from time to time, so they can put their work into context, understand their contribution to the bigger picture, and make informed choices about their work.

Good governance not only requires a formal record of what has happened – which is more important in some contexts than others – but also requires accountable decision making. Your project reports should prompt timely and well-informed decisions from your client, sponsor or project board, which will allow you to proceed at your planned pace. Reports should also give people the information they need, to help resolve issues where you do not have sufficient authority to make the necessary decision, or to secure the resources or funds you need. Finally, they can help you to access the experience or expertise to resolve all of the matters at hand.

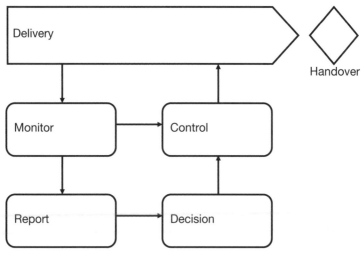

Reporting as part of the monitor and control loop

Change control

One of the commonest complaints of new project leaders is that when they have their project nicely under control, someone will come to them one day, thank them for progress so far, and then say something like 'There's only one thing … I have changed my mind', or 'Something new has cropped up', or 'We need to make some changes.'

It is very tempting to defend your initial scoping work and, for the sake of meeting your deadlines and budget commitments, say something like 'I'm sorry. I'd love to help; but that is not what we agreed.' Such robust assertiveness can really stop scope creep and needless 'nice-to-have' enhancements to functionality that can result in overspend and late delivery. But what if the situation *has* changed, or something *was* missed, and the change you are asked for has real value and is maybe even essential?

Perhaps it is better to say yes. This is, after all, likely to be your first instinct. As a project leader you are a 'can-do' person. But this is equally dangerous. What you need is a process to apply proper control and governance to the request, and get a fully considered decision. This process is called 'change control'.

Step 1: Welcome the change request

When you receive a request for a change in your project, thank the requester for it, and then ask for two things:

1 A precise statement of the change they want. Without this, you can do nothing.

2 A clear statement of why they want it. This should set out the justification for any inconvenience, delay, cost or risk that making the change will cause the project and its sponsoring organisation.

Step 2: Evaluate the change request

Now assess the implications of this change: what it will cost, what resources you will need, what risks are involved, how it will affect other activities, how much time it will need and how much it could delay your project.

Step 3: Get a decision

If you have the authority, make the decision yourself and document your reasons. Otherwise, document a statement of requirements and justifications, and all of your calculations of its impact. Give this to the person or people who do have the authority to make the decision. They can either reject the request (too expensive, risky, disruptive, or not enough benefit) or they can accept it (the benefits or need justify the cost, risk or delay). If the decision is no, then the requester will know that the process has been robust and objective. If it is yes, then you have the authority to commit the extra resources and funds, and incur the increased risk and delay.

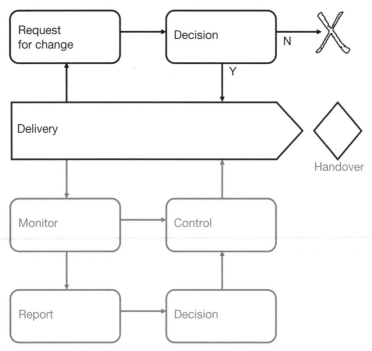

Change control as part of the monitor and control loop

Learning as you go

Some project managers will create a 'lessons learned document' at the end of a project to ensure that their organisation benefits from the knowledge and experience its team has gained. Project leaders know that by focusing on lessons learned throughout the project, not only will their team learn more, but the project will deliver better results.

Start a 'lessons learned' process early on, encouraging a regular discussion at project team meetings of what people have learned and insights they have gained. Open a 'lessons learned log' to record these insights and, importantly, to record and assign consequential actions.

brilliant insight

Too often, what we call 'lessons learned' are really 'lessons identified'. To learn the lesson, we need to internalise it and start to do something differently.

Your lessons learned log should record:

1 What happened.

2 The lesson that was learned from it.

3 Who identified the insight (giving credit is important). It could be two or more people.

4 What consequent changes or actions would apply to the lesson.

5 When the changes or actions should start and be complete (unless ongoing).

6 Who is responsible for ensuring those changes happen.

Use your lessons learned process to notice, share and celebrate successes, as well as correct errors. Growing a body of good practice will give your team, your organisation and you a valuable asset for the future. Most of this book is derived from my own observations and learning of lessons from my own and my peers' good practices, their occasional errors, and my plentiful ones.

Stakeholder leadership in the delivery stage

You should be well into the acting on, reviewing and re-planning of your stakeholder management now; and persistence will pay dividends. The danger you face is getting too caught up internally, in your team and the delivery of your project. Leadership requires pulling back to see not just the whole of your project, but to survey its entire context.

Keep communicating with all of your stakeholders. We will deal in Chapter 10 with what happens when you encounter resistance or conflict, but your best strategy is to avert it, by keeping people informed (an information vacuum leads to gossip and rumours), listening to their concerns, and addressing them promptly, courteously and accurately.

Communicating setbacks

An important part of your role as project leader is to continue to inspire stakeholders and motivate them to support you – especially when your project is facing setbacks. You must remain relentlessly positive and enthusiastic, while retaining objectivity and honesty about your project's status. The way to strike a balance between depressing stakeholders with the stark realities of your problems and leaving them cynical with a naive 'Everything will be fine' message is to set out the following:

1 ***This is how things are***
   Acknowledge the problems and show that you have a strong command of the facts.

2 *This is how things can be*

Spell out how the project can recover and what it will produce, to maintain enthusiasm and motivation.

3 *This is the challenge*

Show your leadership by describing the gap between the two and what you and your team are doing to bridge it.

4 *End with a call to action*

Involve your stakeholders by ending with a request for them to do something to support you, your team and your project. This can be something very small, or a significant contribution, but what it will do is focus them on action and involve them in your problem. The action will give them a sense of control and diminish the feeling of helplessness that can leave stakeholders with a sense of impending project failure.

5 *Close with a final reminder*

... of how things will be when they, you and your team work together.

Your peers as stakeholders

You may also find that you are drawn into competition or disputes with other project leaders, directors or managers, as each of you advocates for your project and the resources you need. You have little to gain and much to lose by letting enthusiastic

> You have little to gain and much to lose by letting enthusiastic competition escalate into conflict.

competition escalate into conflict. They too are stakeholders who can influence your project's outcomes and you may need their help and goodwill one day. Instead, make it your business to support colleagues and peers and find ways to help them out. Building up credit in your 'favours bank' will enable you to draw down on it sometime in the future.

Team leadership in the delivery stage

In Chapter 7, we saw how a team evolves from a random group, through forming, storming and norming, to a cohesive team that is performing at a high level.

But a team can rarely stay at a level of peak performance indefinitely. Peaks and lulls in workload are a natural and inevitable feature of project life and they bring with them tensions that can leave your team out of kilter.

Diagnosing the problem

A high-performing team is one where two things are nicely balanced: team members know, value and work hard at their work tasks, and at the same time they collaborate effectively and care

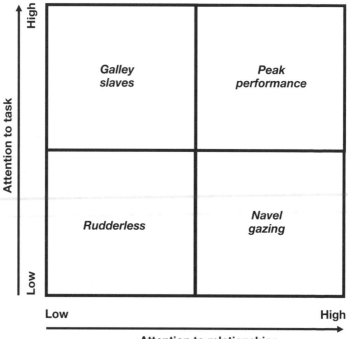

Team performance

for one another. This gives us two axes of concern: task and relationship. When one suffers, the team performance takes a dip and, if it suffers for too long, troubles will be afoot. If you are able to spot what is happening and act accordingly, you will be able to lead your team back to high performance.

Galley slaves

Perhaps the more likely scenario with a project team is that a peak of work continues for so long that people start to feel stressed by the relentless pressure. They feel like slaves chained to their oar in a Roman galley, with no escape from their daily toil. Unsurprisingly, they feel they have little time or energy for the person on the bench next to them, much less the one three rows down. Tempers start to fray, spontaneous collaboration diminishes and initiative with it. Only pressure from you keeps driving them on.

To refresh your team, you need to take time out to rebuild relationships. Social activities will remind everyone of how much they liked and respected their colleagues, so take off the pressure for a short while and let people relax and reconnect with one another. You will find a palpable change in the atmosphere very quickly.

Navel gazing

Sometimes there is a little lull in activity that can give people a bit of a breather. But if that lull lasts for too long, people will start to get bored. What we do when we get bored – just like a toddler – is we make mischief. It will start with too much time to chat, resulting in stronger relationships, but eventually, that chat can turn toxic, focusing on the project's shortcomings, or the organisation's, or yours. Eventually people will criticise colleagues and then those criticisms will get around and the atmosphere will become poisonous. If you are not careful, the stronger relationships will weaken and, with little work to do and poor relationships, your team will disintegrate into a rudderless state with no sense of direction.

Work is important, so if there is a delay, find something to keep your team busy. Ideally it will be valuable, meaningful work but, frankly, if there is none to be had, create some work or take a day out for the whole team to do some voluntary service – which is valuable and meaningful in a different way.

Rudderless

If you do find your team rudderless, then you could in principle rebuild it by starting on the relationships or by focusing on work. My experience is that the task-focus route is quicker and more certain. It is the way we form teams in the first place, so feels more comfortable to team members. Working together on a challenge is a great way to re-strengthen old relationships.

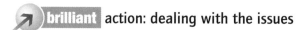 **action: dealing with the issues**

A dip in enthusiasm, leading to cynicism, leading to mistrust and then blame and personal attacks is a route you will passionately want to avoid. Here are seven tips to help you tackle a dysfunctional team.

1 Remind them what it is all for

Go back to the things that inspired the team at the start: your goal and the difference your project's outcomes will make.

2 Give them the speech

The five steps of how to communicate a setback in the previous section will work as well for your team as it will for your stakeholders.

3 Shake things up

If things aren't working, you have nothing to lose by doing things differently. Ask for innovation and creative thinking, reallocate team members to new roles, restructure your plan, or simply make cosmetic changes to your environment and where people work.

4 Bring in outsiders

Either introduce new people into the project or take the team to another project in a different organisation in a new sector, to see what they do and identify new ideas and ways of doing things.

5 Learn something new

Create training or other learning opportunities for your team – together – to refresh their perspectives and find new ways to do things.

6 Create success

Success is motivating, so create opportunities for the team to celebrate, by focusing on small wins that the team can make quickly.

7 Bring in someone inspirational

Get a senior leader from your organisation or an inspirational figure from outside to come and visit your project, meet your team and sprinkle some magic dust on them.

If all else fails, it can be time for a big change: changing some team members or even, if you are confident that it is the right thing, the project leader.

Handover

As your project nears its end, you will feel a desire to get it finished, hand it over and move on to the next thing. However, completion to

> If it isn't right, it isn't finished.

agreed quality standards and an orderly handover to the new beneficial owners of your deliverables are partly a matter of character. If it isn't right, it isn't finished.

Testing and evaluation may be a formal part of your project management process, but if it is not, it will still pay you to convene some form of pre-handover review, with key team members and one or two outsiders contributing to an assessment of how you have met the requirements of your contract or project definition.

Take the lead in focusing attention on corrective actions rather than blamefinding and close the review with a last check of the handover arrangements, to make sure that nothing will go wrong and that all risks are addressed.

The final handover and agreement of any snagging items that need to be addressed afterwards are not something that I would delegate. They are an important part of managing your relationships with essential stakeholders, and what you are handing over is fundamentally responsibility: you are responsible for the deliverables and you are seeking for the new custodian to accept full responsibility.

Brilliant delivery

Creating a brilliant project during the delivery stage is all about your team's successes along the way. Use each milestone as an opportunity to celebrate, so they stay motivated and the good news leaks out. Promote these successes using all appropriate media, like in-house magazines and newsletters, so that your project builds a sense of momentum among the wider stakeholder group.

Finally, keep things fresh by looking for and harnessing 'Eureka!' moments that can transform how your team works and take their knowledge and insight to a higher level. A brilliant project is fun to contribute to, so foster a light-hearted working style to get a serious focus on the work.

brilliant recap

- With your planning done, it is time to hand over delivery to your team.

- The monitor and control loop is the heart of the delivery phase: stay in touch with everything that is happening and address issues quickly.

- Welcome ideas for change, but evaluate each rigorously, on its merits.

- Learn as you go – give credit for innovation and good practice, and spread the new ideas widely.

- Keep communicating with your stakeholders to keep them engaged. Don't hide bad news: share it and remain optimistic.

- Be aware of the state of your team's motivation and act to repair any damage to its performance.

- Take responsibility for handover, because responsibility is precisely what you are handing over.

CHAPTER 9

Project closure stage

S ome projects seem to never end even though there is nothing else to do. As with a dripping tap, you can't seem to turn them off, so they persist, draining you of emotional energy. Wouldn't it be great just to close them?

Experienced project managers know that handover is just the start of the closure stage. To finish the project, they must discipline themselves and their team to complete three last tasks. Project leaders know that they must also mark this ending and prepare their people for the next beginning: project life is a series of cycles.

Three tasks

Handover marks not just the end of the delivery stage of your project, but also the start of the closure stage. The closure stage ends with a formal statement that the project is closed – which used to be called a 'project closure memo'. But who writes memos these days? Even so, a formal meeting note, contractual letter, exchange of emails or a completed pro forma placed at the end of your project file will clearly indicate that you and your boss, client or sponsor agree that the project is complete and nothing further is needed.

Between handover and project closure memo, there are three things that project managers must attend to.

1. Review

The project manager must conduct a number of reviews and each of these presents an opportunity also to lead. We will examine these in more detail in the next section.

2. Administration

Most projects involve a lot of admin and there will be many loose ends to tie up. The unappealing nature of admin to most project managers – whose personalities tend to prefer getting things started – is one of the chief reasons for the dripping tap syndrome.

Project leaders know their teams and will recognise if any members are particularly good at getting admin tasks finished, with the i's dotted and the t's crossed. Back in Chapter 2, we saw that Belbin described this team role as the 'completer-finisher'. If you have such individuals, use them. If you don't, you may have a junior member of the team who could benefit from taking on a responsibility and here is a last opportunity for you to give them one, on this project. If all else fails, remind the team that, until they clear all of the necessary project admin, they cannot have the third thing …

3. Celebration

Always celebrate the end of your project. This marks your team's success and will help everyone to recognise the work they have done and feel good about their contribution. This will build their confidence, leading to better performance in future, which will lead to stronger results too. Stronger results create more success, offering more opportunity to celebrate. Hurrah: a virtuous cycle!

> Stronger results create more success, offering more opportunity to celebrate.

What to review

There are always three core things to review at the end of your project, and there may be others depending on the nature of your particular project. We will start with:

1 Project review

2 Lessons learned

3 Individual feedback.

You will always need to do these – although you may often combine the first two into one process with one output. Some projects may also benefit from one or more of these:

4 Outcomes review

5 Customer review

6 Sponsor review

7 Team review.

1. Project review

How well did the project succeed in delivering its planned products? How well did you meet your time, cost and quality objectives? How did your team perform? How successful were your processes and procedures? How would you assess the management and leadership? How effective and accountable were the governance arrangements? These questions and more can be answered in a structured review – either among the project team or conducted by outsiders.

Leadership can transform your project review from a mundane administrative necessity to a process and resulting products that are thought provoking and transformational. Do not satisfy yourself with bare facts: look at impacts on your organisation or your client's organisation, and the people concerned. Find ways to present the information so that key people can really get the significance of what your project has done: seminars, keynote presentations, videos, magazines, for example. Think innovatively about how your project review can support the project itself in making a real difference. The same can also be true of number two ...

2. Lessons learned

A lot of people are sceptical at best, ranging to downright cynical, about structured lessons learned reviews. They observe that few produce anything new and fewer still make it into the reading lists of the senior people who could make change happen in their organisations.

This misses a large part of the point: the people with most to learn from a lessons learned review are the project team members themselves. Reflecting on their accumulated lessons learned log and discussing what happened and why, and each person's thoughts, can give each team member a valuable set of stories, tools and insights to take to their next project.

Here is a real opportunity for leadership. If you adopt a learning attitude and are open to feedback and frank discussion of your actions and decisions, then others will feel freer to do the same. You must ensure that the atmosphere is a constructive one that seeks reasons to credit people with success and innovation, and gives no blame for mistakes. Rather, mistakes are opportunities to learn about process and review evidence. To do this, you must set a tone of honesty about what really happened.

3. Individual feedback

A real leadership task that is often transformed into a management imperative by organisational procedures is giving performance feedback to each team member. But don't do it because you have to: do it because it is right. Give feedback to your team members in the spirit of one last personal act of leadership to those individuals. Here is your chance to thank them personally for their contribution, acknowledge and celebrate their personal successes, help them to draw out individual lessons, and prepare them for their next role.

brilliant example: cascade feedback

In one large project I worked on, my team numbered 60 or so, but was divided into five work streams, some of which had sub-teams with team leaders. I sat down with each work-stream leader and spent an hour or so discussing their role at the end of the project. They then cascaded that process with their teams.

Our agenda was informal – we met over coffee and a Danish pastry, I recall. Each meeting covered six things:

1 Thank you for your help.

2 What things I particularly appreciated in your work and personal style.

3 What things are you most proud of? I encouraged multiple answers.

4 What did you feel did not go so well? We discussed what we could each learn, and what feedback they might need to pass on.

5 What opportunities would you like to look for next? We focused on the future and on our joint assessment of how they could best create that opportunity and what preparation they would need to make. In some contexts, you may want to offer your assessment of what they could look for next.

6 Closing assessment. I reiterated my thanks and my commitments to any agreed actions to support them in the future, and I wished them well.

4. Outcomes review

Assessing your project's deliverables at your project review will give no indication of their benefit to your business, client group or customer. They will need to be used in operational service for a period of time before you can evaluate whether their anticipated benefits are being realised and the outcomes that the organisation is achieving match those it hoped for at the start of your project. This will take time, so all you can do in the closure stage is schedule your outcomes review.

The longer you wait, the more evidence you will have, so the more robust your conclusions will be. On the other hand, the sooner you do the review, the sooner you can address any shortcomings in the operational implementation or the design of your deliverables. Leadership is about judgement, so balance these two pressures to find the right time frame for your outcomes review. Typically, this will be from six to 18 months after handover – no less than three months. Err on the shorter side, unless you know that a full operational cycle will be needed to gain enough data, and that cycle time is longer.

Think carefully about who will best be able to contribute to the review and put it in people's diaries now, while the project is still live.

5. Customer review

If your project has been done for a customer or client, you may want to create a customer review where you can get their direct feedback on your work. This is a chance to address concerns before they can become commercially toxic, and cement good relationships for the future. You may also find it offers the chance to discuss future projects – maybe related to the one you have completed.

Here is a prime opportunity to practise your listening skills. Avoid becoming defensive about criticism, and accept compliments with grace and humility. Offer your recognition and thanks for your customer's support and the contributions of their own staff. If your relationship and feedback are both strong, you can also ask for a testimonial.

6. Sponsor review

If your client is internal, then you may want to conduct a similar review with your project sponsor. This can focus on either your project performance or on your own personal performance as project leader. If you want to cover both, I recommend making a clear dividing line in your meeting.

7. Team review

You may also want to review team working with your project team. This is of most value where team members are likely to work with one another again in future teams, or if a large chunk of your team will move to a new project together. It is a chance to solidify effective team processes, re-examine any that don't work, and clear the air over any tensions or conflict.

If your team is going to split up, you can use this review as a part of the 'mourning' process.

Mourning

In the 1960s, Bruce Tuckman developed his Forming, Storming, Norming, Performing model of team development. In 1977, with co-researcher Mary Ann Jensen, he reviewed his work and they concluded that they had missed a phase, which is crucial for project leaders to understand.

Tuckman and Jensen realised that when the team split up, a new process happened, so they labelled this new stage 'Adjourning'. However, many people now give this phase the alternative name of 'Mourning'. I favour this, not because I am crass enough to believe that this is as powerful an event in our lives as real mourning, but because it does seem to trigger the same kind

> A team that has really performed will enjoy each other's company and feel proud of their achievements.

of emotions, and because the things you need to do as a project leader are similar to the things we do when we mourn.

A team that has really performed will enjoy each other's company and feel proud of their achievements. There will be strong bonds of respect and often friendship. Just going their separate ways at the end of the project will feel wrong, and leave an emotional gap. So, as cultures do to mark a death, before you think ahead about 'What next?' you should make time to mark the transition. Take time with your team to acknowledge that you are losing something special, and celebrate what you have achieved together. This will help all of you to move on.

Transforming

As a project leader in an organisation that did little more than a series of projects, I observed that many project teams did not just disband. A few team members might leave this project and many would move together to the next one. But they would have different roles, there would be new team members and a new environment to adapt to, and hierarchies would shift. The team had transformed. My observation was that the new team – although substantially like the old – would rarely slip straight back into performing mode.

Sometimes, with a small change, people would focus on the work and try to figure out how the team would accommodate the changes and find new norms: it had reverted to the norming stage.

Sometimes, the new team members caused frictions, or there was competition for roles or for seniority. Team members might also seek to influence a new leader or expert. This focus on getting the relationships right reminded me of the storming stage.

Sometimes the new work was significantly different, or the new team members changed everything. Many new relationships had to be forged and new skills and roles had to be developed. The team had slid all the way back to the forming stage.

When your team transforms, for whatever reason, be aware that it may revert to an earlier stage of the Tuckman life cycle. Stay alert for the signs that will tell you which stage it is now in and, critically, adapt your leadership style to the new stage. If you continue a light-touch performing stage style of leadership for a team that is storming, little work will get done, you will fail to harness the creative energy, your leadership will seem weak, and some team members may feel threatened and uncomfortable.

Brilliant closure

The closure stage is your last chance to make your project brilliant. It is also your last chance to treat your team outstandingly well at team and individual levels. Get your feedback right by taking real care over how you prepare and conduct all of your reviews. Details matter, and this will leave people with the impression that you led them well, to the very end of the project. The alternative is that you turn your attention to your next project and people come away feeling a little abandoned, which can take the shine off the brilliance of this project. People remember beginnings and endings. A bad ending can wipe out a project load of investment in brilliance.

On the other hand, a spectacular ending can really put the shine on a good project. Celebration is the key. Celebrate your project publicly, and with your team. Find a celebration that is appropriate to the culture of your team and your organisation and that is consistent in scale with your project. It does not need to be costly or lavish: what matters is the spirit with which you plan it.

 **brilliant** recap

- Don't let your project run on like a dripping tap. Close it down in an orderly manner.

- The three essential closure actions are reviewing, admin and celebration.

- Use your project reviews as a chance to demonstrate leadership.

- Recognise your team's emotional need to mark the end of their project.

- Plan and execute a suitable celebration of your completed project.

PART 3

Project team
leadership in
tough times

I n tough times, project management is not enough. People get scared and uncertain and need leadership to keep them working effectively. Now you must focus a substantial part of your energies on giving people confidence and keeping them motivated to work through the adversity.

This will take all of your social skills and we'll examine the skills you will need in the two most challenging scenarios, resistance and crisis, in Chapters 10 and 11. In the final chapter, we will focus on you, and your personal skills of resilience, influence and taking care of yourself.

It is in tough times that leaders are really judged. Therefore, they are good tests of your abilities and you should welcome them. This is not to say that you will enjoy them, so don't create the conditions to invite tough times.

Some say leadership is lonely and, in tough times, this is certainly true. Regrets and recriminations are useless: you will have to accept what is, accept responsibility for it, and deal with it. You will doubtless get advice from many sources, which you should accept. But only you will be responsible for the ultimate decisions.

In tough times, you must balance compassion for your people with clear-thinking objectivity about the situation. You won't always get it right, but the mark of a true leader is their ability to learn and respond flexibly. This is what Part 3 is about.

CHAPTER 10

Tough times: meeting resistance

Projects create change, and change inevitably brings about resistance. Even when the change is manifestly beneficial, there is a tendency to be suspicious of the motives behind it, or to suspect that it is not what it seems. The source of our resistance is in our minds: we may be fearful of the change or of our ability to cope with it; we may know we can cope, but not want to make the effort; we may want to make the effort, but be sceptical about whether it will be worthwhile.

Why change leads to resistance

Our response to change is part of how our brain works. We can see it in how we react to a physical threat. Our first response is that of a startled hedgehog facing a fox: we freeze. By refusing to engage with the threat, it may pass without bothering us. This is not effective when the two bright lights are not reflections from the eyes, but the lights of a truck.

The structure of resistance

However, we have all experienced the hope that, if I don't look now, my car may not be scratched, my phone may not be broken, or the injury may be slight. We do the same when confronted by change and put it out of our mind and try and carry on as normal. This is 'denial'.

Once we engage with the threat – or the change – our mind moves us into 'fight-or-flight' mode. A scared gazelle will run from a threat: a cornered bear will take it on. In this mode, our thinking is dominated by the instinctive and emotional parts of our brain. Hence, when facing change, we often get angry, upset, scared, frustrated or embittered. You will experience all of these emotions, and many more, from other people when leading change.

Because people's thought processes are dominated by emotion, reason becomes subordinate, so there is little point in trying to explain, or asking them not to be angry or upset: it will just make things worse. The only thing you can do is allow the emotion to subside.

Resistance is rational. It is the conscious stand against the change, where people find a dozen good reasons why the change is foolish, dangerous or just wrong. The reality is that they are probably, in part, right. Organisational change is complex, and if everything your project is designed to do is manifestly beneficial to everyone, then you would not expect resistance. But in the real world, there will be compromises and constraints that mean your project will have consequences for some. These can be complicated and unattractive.

> in the real world, there will be compromises and constraints that mean your project will have consequences

So welcome the resistance as a chance to learn about the effects of your project on different stakeholders, and see it as a part of the process; not as a threat to it.

Beyond resistance

Wait until you meet rational resistance before making your counter arguments, because they will remain unheard if you make them when I am angry, upset and emotional. If you make them at the right time, if you make them well and, most important, if your arguments have substance, you will start to win me round. The rational part of me will start to explore the benefits of the changes your project is introducing and I will come to understand why I should support it. If you now allow me enough time, I will come to accept the change emotionally too. For some people, in some circumstances, this can be very quick. At other times, it can take weeks, months, or even years.

Timing and leadership

This sequence of denial followed by an emotional response, followed by a rational resistance, followed by a rational exploration, followed by an emotional acceptance is universal, as long as the reasons to accept the change do outweigh the reasons to reject it. What differs from person to person, and between situations, is how we each express ourselves at each stage and how long we need to work through the stages.

Good leadership means giving people the resources and time they need, so they can move through each stage. By dealing appropriately with the response you encounter, you can hasten people's progress, but if you try to rush them, you will entrench anger, fear and resistance.

Move people from denial by giving them the evidence they need to evaluate the situation for themselves. When they become emotional, respect their emotions and allow them to express those emotions as they choose. There is nothing worse than saying something like 'There's no point in getting angry …' Far better to say something like 'I can see how angry you are. Can you tell me more about what is making you feel this way?'

This sort of response has two positive effects. First, it clearly respects my anger, and second, it will encourage me to reflect on my anger, shifting my focus from the emotion to analysis, so moving me towards a rational articulation of my resistance. When reasoned resistance dominates, you can then start to address my concerns.

Handling resistance to change

Mike's second rule of change

Always respect your resisters.

People resist change for a reason, so your job is to find that reason and address it. This means listening carefully to how they express themselves, to learn more about their concerns and what you need to say or do to counter them. There are five principal reasons why people resist change.

I don't understand *why* we need to change

This level of resistance comes when people fail to see the triggering events that have caused your project to be commissioned. Your project therefore seems pointless and a waste of time and resources. To counter this resistance, you need to find compelling evidence that external changes or pressures mean that a response – in the form of your project – is absolutely necessary.

I don't understand why *this* change

Now they understand that change is necessary, but you need to make a stronger case that your project is the right response to the external factors that demand change. It may be that you have not articulated your case well enough, and they simply don't find it compelling, or it may be that they have misunderstood your case, and you are, effectively, speaking at cross purposes.

I don't *like* this change

This is, perhaps, the most important level of resistance, and there are two possible causes.

Subjective

At a personal level, it is perfectly reasonable for me to resist a change if I am going to be worse off as a result. In the real world, many organisations are forced to make changes that, while making overall improvements, can leave some casualties – people for whom the change really is adverse. If you conclude that I am among those people, then there is only one response you can offer with integrity. You must recognise my situation and offer help and resources as far as you are able to, to support me in making the decisions I will need to make. The worst thing you can do is try to diminish or gloss over my situation. We will see the long-term consequences of this behaviour soon.

Objective

Sometimes I will argue that I don't like the change, not because of how it affects me, but because of how I perceive it will affect the organisation. I think that what you are doing, or how you are doing it, is wrong. I may be right or wrong in my assessment, but as a leader, you must listen to me carefully and make an objective assessment of my insights. If all that you do is sideline me and I turn out to be right, then you have failed. If you listen to me, evaluate my evidence with care, and then conclude I am wrong, then you have fulfilled your leadership role – even if you make the wrong decision.

I don't like *change*

Some people just don't like change. In fact, if you push anybody far enough, you will reach their threshold of fear, where the level of change leaves them afraid that they won't be able to cope. Two things could be going on. At the less intense emotional level, they could be saying 'I don't *know how* to change.' If this is your diagnosis, your role is to find ways to prepare them for life once your project delivers, combining support, training and guidance.

At a deeper level, they may be saying 'I don't *believe* I can change.' You must address this lack of confidence by undermining it. It is just a belief, so help them to find evidence that contradicts it. For example:

● What changes have they encountered before, that they thought they could not cope with, but did?

● Who is there that is like them, who has adapted to this change successfully?

I don't like *you*

One thing everyone knows about times of change is that there will be resistance. So if I want to kick back at you, your team, the organisation or the world in general, what better time to do this than now? I can disguise my enmity as resistance. If this is the case, then you do not have to indulge me – this is a form of misbehaviour and you should deal with it accordingly.

The onion model

The five levels of resistance we have discussed are like the layers of an onion. When you peel one off, there are more beneath – and each gets hotter than the last. The figure opposite illustrates the onion model of resistance.

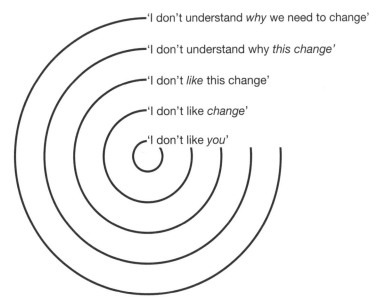

'I don't understand *why* we need to change'

'I don't understand why *this change*'

'I don't *like* this change'

'I don't like *change*'

'I don't like *you*'

The onion model of resistance

Mike's third rule of change

Some people will welcome the change. Make them your allies.

Divide and rule

When a group of people shares a point of view, they tend to reinforce one another's arguments and, thereby, strengthen their beliefs. Group-think is the process whereby a group fails to evaluate new information, focusing on 'what we all know' instead. Consequently, people who are resistant to your project will seek out like-minded allies and strengthen their resistance.

There will always be some people who will support your project; make them your allies. Engage them in advocating for your project, because they can be more effective than you can. If you say your project is a good one, your partisanship will dilute your argument. If you can get me to advocate for you, my independence will give my point of view greater weight.

Try to separate your detractors and resisters, and allocate your supporters to each. Prepare your advocates with up-to-date briefings and prepared arguments, and periodically debrief them to understand the nature of the resistance they are facing. Evaluate it for valid concerns and make changes to your project if necessary. Publicise these changes to show that you are, indeed, listening. This will give the sense that changes which you do not make are less valid.

Understanding misbehaviour

The 'I don't like *you*' level of resistance can sometimes turn into an entrenched pattern of behaviour that constantly repeats itself. Stephen Karpman analysed these repetitive patterns of behaviour – sometimes known as 'games' – to create a simple model that helps us understand what is going on: the 'drama triangle'.

When one of us misbehaves, they take a position at one corner of the triangle, forcing the other into another corner. As the game continues, one of us will switch positions, creating an emotional pay-off. Let's look at three examples.

Example 1: 'How dare you?'

In this game, your resister takes an aggressive 'persecutor' role and challenges you over your actions, forcing you into a victim role. This makes them feel good because they have the power in the relationship. If you try to regain power by assertively defending yourself, the resister can slip into the victim role and feel good by casting you as a bully, or come to your rescue and regain their power by making you feel dependent upon their support.

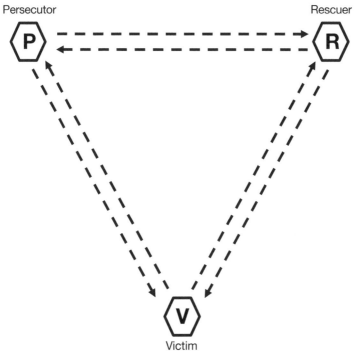

Persecutor   Rescuer

Victim

The drama triangle

Example 2: 'Poor me'

Where the resister casts themself as a 'victim', you are forced into the persecutor role. This feels uncomfortable and your easiest way out – the one the resister would love – is for you to become their rescuer and accede to their wishes. If you don't do this, they may want to offer you a deal which allows them to rescue you, but can leave you feeling like a victim.

Example 3: 'Let me help you'

A more covert form of resistance is to try and subvert your plans by starting from the 'rescuer' position. Here the resister presupposes that you are in trouble and that your project is wrong in some way, and offers to help you out. The danger is that you accept the presupposition uncritically, because it feels good to be cared for in this way. It casts you as victim. If, however, you resist this casting and defend your project, saying it needs no rescuing, the resister will revert to a victim role and accuse you of bullying tactics.

Breaking out of the drama triangle

If any of these scenarios feel scarily familiar, you have been trapped in games. There is no way to win them, because the very playing of them is dysfunctional. The only way out is to stop playing: to say something like 'This feels like a conversation we've had before; let's talk about it', or 'I don't think we are approaching this discussion fruitfully, let's look at things another way.' If all else fails, politely refuse to engage in a no-win conversation.

Resolving conflict

When you find yourself in conflict, there are three things to address:

● The personal dimension
● The substance of the conflict
● The resolution process.

A sound process can rebuild relationships and address the substance of the conflict.

Step 1: Personal engagement

De-escalating conflict starts when you make a decision to engage in a positive and respectful manner. Demonstrate that you understand the other person's concerns – or at least that they have them – and show appreciation for their first steps in engaging with you to resolve your shared conflict.

Step 2: Sharing the substance

You need to understand each other's points of view and work

from a shared basis of facts about
the situation, your definitions, your
emotional responses to it, and your
concerns and hopes. Work together,
uncritically, to itemise all of the rel-

Acknowledge the value of each other's opinions

evant facts and feelings and take care to distinguish facts from
opinions. Acknowledge the value of each other's opinions, whilst
agreeing that they need to be assessed against the evidence.

Step 3: Decide what resolution will look like

Discuss your respective requirements for a good resolution. This
may not be for agreement – remember that it is the conflict you
need to resolve and you may not be able to agree on the substantive matter. State your joint commitment to work together
towards a resolution:

● What were you committed to do?

● What do you now commit to do?

Step 4: Explore options

What resources do you have? What do you agree on? What is
missing? What are the possibilities for creating agreed solutions?

Step 5: Negotiate a resolution

Make offers and counter offers to move towards an agreement
for next steps and promises to one another.

---

brilliant tactics: ten tips for resolving conflict

1   Distinguish the person from the problem. Even if you detest their
    behaviour, continue to respect them.

2   Practise intense listening, and wait until you have heard the whole
    message before framing your response.

▶

3   Use the power of silence to encourage them to say more. How people interpret a silence often betrays their own doubts.

4   Check and recheck your understanding of their feelings, opinions and position, to avoid compounding the conflict with further misunderstanding.

5   To help reduce personal conflict, avoid using the word 'you', which can sound accusatory or as if you know what I am thinking. Use the word 'I' to take responsibility for your opinions, interpretations and actions.

6   If the conflict is about opinions and interpretation, rather than facts, consider getting other stakeholders involved to introduce more opinions and thus reduce the tension, and to see if weight of opinion can change the other person's mind – or yours.

7   Look for information or data that one party is missing. This will give them a face-saving chance to re-evaluate their position, rather than change their mind.

8   Make positive commitments to change or to actions that underscore your personal sense of responsibility for resolving the conflict.

9   If you realise you are wrong, own up to it immediately and take responsibility for your error. Put progress ahead of pride.

10 And also put progress before pride in granting credit for ideas that move you forward – whether they are yours or not.

brilliant recap

- Resistance to change is inevitable – it is part of our normal response to it.

- Respect the people who resist and learn what you can from their resistance.

- There are five principal reasons why people resist. If you can diagnose the resistance you are getting, you can handle it effectively.

- Use supporters of your project as advocates to help win over resisters.

- People who misbehave often get into a cycle that you can understand with the drama triangle.

- Follow a structured five-step process to help you resolve conflict.

CHAPTER 11

Tough times:
up against it

S hift happens. Things go wrong.

There is a saying: 'What is, is' which some people interpret as fatalistic, inferring that we cannot change things. A project leader cannot afford such a luxury. You must accept what has happened with equanimity, and then deal with it.

When things go wrong, focus forward on understanding the situation, identifying what you can do about it, and acting to bring it under control.

What to do when something goes wrong

I was nearing the end of my daily monitoring meetings with work-stream leaders. The next one I saw had worrying news – a significant problem with a deliverable that was due in 24 hours. Because I was up-to-date with the project, I was able to drop everything to turn my attention to his problem.

If you are in control of your project – constantly monitoring status and aware of everything that happens – then you are in an ideal position to handle problems. When something

> When something goes wrong you need to address the issue rapidly

goes wrong you need to be able to address the issue rapidly, and also act to calm your team, so they can contribute effectively.

The SCOPE process

The SCOPE process is a five-step process for mentally taking control of a situation.

Stop   Mentally and physically pause. Avoid rushing in.

Clarify   Seek out all relevant facts that will help you understand the situation and its potential consequences.

Options   Identify alternative options for your response, and evaluate each against potential consequences. Select your course of action.

Proceed   Now act decisively.

Evaluate   Review outcomes against your evaluation and, if you are not getting the results you expected, Stop, Clarify, select a new Option …

Keep your team involved

When something goes wrong, speak with your team and let them know the situation. In the absence of information, rumours will cause greater uncertainty and will quickly undermine morale, confidence and effectiveness. Keep the team busy, because idleness feels like impotence and people will have nothing to do but talk about how bad things are. When we are working on a solution, however, we feel in control: stress levels are lower and morale is higher. Your ideal mood will be one of calm determination, a sense of urgency without panic and a commitment to resolving the problem.

Keep stakeholders informed

There is less that your stakeholders will be able to do, so keeping them informed to stifle unhelpful rumours will be even more important. This will feel like a low priority, but it is not. So if you feel unable to dedicate the time needed, delegate the role to a spokesperson, who is closely involved with your team's work and can speak authoritatively, and keep them well informed. Frequently agree with them what messages to communicate, and how.

Deal with the problem

There is a wealth of problem-solving tools that work well in a project environment. Synthesising the best of them leads to a ten-step plan. Adapt this plan to your own environment

↗ brilliant tactics

1 Do what is necessary to prevent more danger or damage.

2 Identify what has happened.

3 Examine the causes.

4 Determine what needs to be done in the long term.

5 Review your options for effecting the change.

6 Decide which option is best.

7 Plan how to get that option implemented as quickly and cost-effectively as is safe.

8 Consider how to secure the project so that the same thing cannot happen again.

9 Establish what you can learn from the situation systemically, and how each individual concerned can best incorporate the lessons into their professional practice.

10 Celebrate the successful closure of the issue.

Time, cost, quality

All crises will put pressure on one or more corners of the time–cost–quality triangle – usually on all of them. Your leadership role is to determine your relative priorities for protecting schedule, budget and outcome, knowing that one at least must be sacrificed to protect the others. For example, with a fixed deadline, you will have to sacrifice budget, outcomes or both, or with a fixed specification, you will have to spend more or accept delays, or both.

Whilst there may be flexibility in your budget, it is rarely an option to spend your way out of trouble and protect both schedule and deliverables, so you will nearly always end up spending a little more, making some difficult decisions about compromising your deliverables, and putting your timetable on the line.

Crashing the deadlines

The term 'crashing the deadlines' refers to the set of actions you can take to speed your project along, either to advance delivery or, more often, to catch up after a serious delay. All of the compromises and concessions that this will require of you and your team will be uncomfortable and all will bear some risk. Leadership is about choosing which to pursue and keeping team members motivated yet under control.

Defining the work

No matter how pressing your deadlines, you must always define your outcomes with absolute clarity. In times of pressure, you can least afford nugatory work resulting from an ill-defined result. However, the individual task definitions that may be rigorously planned at the outset of a well-managed project can be left far vaguer when under pressure, allowing team members to find pragmatic solutions to creating the required outcomes.

Agreeing the way forward

When you have the luxury of time, you may favour a democratic process for finding and agreeing solutions to problems – aiming for wide consensus – before sign-off. If you are in a rush, that consensus will go, in favour of your confidence as a leader and the required sign-off. When you are under maximum time pressure, even sign-offs can be abandoned as long as there is sufficient discussion with the people in authority to create trust on both sides.

When it comes to planning how to implement your solutions, you will increasingly tolerate gaps in the detail of plans and, at full speed, may be prepared to work with nothing more than a framework plan, coupled with the instincts and experience of your team members. One area where your plan will help is in prioritising tasks that are most important, or are on your critical path, and possibly setting aside or delaying other activities.

Resources

Your carefully managed budget may be an early casualty of a rush job and you will also seek additional authorised expenditure. When crashing timelines completely, you may even be prepared to sacrifice a measure of normal budgetary control and abandon some of your previous cost priorities. This will be one of the hardest judgements to make, because relinquishing strong budgetary control has significant risk. Ideally, you will have the resources to fully manage your spending and get regular, properly authorised injections of extra funds.

You may also have to make the resources you have work harder – known as 'sweating your assets'. This means your team will need to work harder and any additional people who are available are called in and deployed. Introducing additional resources to a crisis situation can help or hinder. The SWAT or Tiger Team approach of bringing in an extra group of specialists can create new energy but alienate your core team. New team members can be a drain on resources as existing members need to brief and support them. Their well-meaning feedback on how things are done can sap morale and slow the team down.

Often, project team members within organisations need to integrate their project activity into a wide set of competing priorities. As your project comes under pressure, you will increasingly ask them to prioritise this activity. At the limit, you will need them to put all else aside. Consider using overtime and extended working hours.

Attitudes

With the focusing of resources on your project, your and their commitment to getting the job done will become a single-minded focus that can tend towards tunnel vision. If your team succumbs to tunnel vision, that is fine; as long as you do not. It is imperative to lift your sights to the horizon and scan in all directions from time to time. Nowhere is this more relevant than in the domain of risk.

> If your team succumbs to tunnel vision, that is fine; as long as you do not.

In a normal project, you will set your risk thresholds carefully to minimise risk in the context of budgetary constraints and your desire to innovate. As time pressure increases, there can be a tendency to accept greater risks, but you must take time to calculate these risks and only accept them knowingly. Only under the severest pressure, with little to lose, can you set aside such caution and incur significant risks.

Contingency planning

Risk management is an essential component of any project management process. Fundamentally, it consists of five components.

Identify   Identify all potential risks.

Analyse   Assess the risks for likelihood, impact and other relevant characteristics, such as proximity (how soon they may impact) and triggering incidents.

Plan   Develop a plan to manage the risk.

Action   Execute your plan.

Monitor and control

Your plan may consist of a combination of mitigating actions designed to reduce the likelihood or impact of the risk, or transfer of its impact to one or other third party (insurance is an example). You may also plan to accept the risk and deal with the consequences, should they arise. For high-impact threats, however, you will usually only consider accepting a risk in this way if you also plan for how you will deal with it, in advance. This plan is called a 'contingency plan' or sometimes, colloquially, as a 'Plan B'.

Developing a contingency plan

Three components feed into a contingency plan:

1 **Scenarios**
   Survey the possible scenarios that can play out and select a small number of representative examples that carry the breadth of possibilities. Examine what triggers or leading indicators might alert you to which scenario will be realised.

2 **Consequences**
   In each of your working scenarios, what are the potential impacts on service, delivery, regulation, revenue, people, environment, timelines, costs? These will help you to prioritise actions to protect the things that are most at risk.

3 **Resources**
   What people, assets, materials, insurances and back-up systems do you have available? What elements of functionality could you abandon safely and still achieve your core goal?

Define and document a plan that answers all of the questions: what, where, when, who and how. Constrain your plan by understanding the breadth of your objectives: whether it is containment of the worst consequences or complete recovery of your project. Define responsibilities and, because you will be working under crisis conditions, document your plan in an easy-to-follow, step-by-step format.

Readiness

Keep your contingency plans under review, and constantly scan for indicators that one of your adverse scenarios is becoming likely.

brilliant recap

- Shift happens, so accept it and deal with it.
- SCOPE the problem, keep your team and stakeholders informed, and deal with the issue in a structured way.
- Crises will impact on one or more of time, cost and quality. Make a conscious decision about which to protect and which to sacrifice.
- When you need to crash the deadlines, make pragmatic choices about how you relax controls on definitions, planning, budgets and risk, while increasing the effort you expect of your team.
- Preparedness means having contingency plans to deal with the realisation of significant risks.

CHAPTER 12

Tough times:
tough leader

Leadership is not easy day to day, but it is in tough times that you will really be tested. Now you must set a personal example, inspiring your team while controlling your own anxieties and concerns. The difficult balance to strike is in sharing the reality of any problems with your team while remaining calm and optimistic so that your team feels a sense that you are in control.

Tough times call for some extraordinary resources, and we will look at four areas:

1 *Resilience*: your ability to remain objective and effective under pressure.

2 *Emotional leadership*: your ability to engage your team and inspire confidence in them.

3 *Political leadership*: your ability to get things done within a social and organisational setting.

4 *Staying tough*: your ability to look after your own physical and emotional well-being.

Resilience

Your ability to cope with setbacks – both personal and professional – and to perform well in adverse conditions – is called 'resilience'. There are three vital attitudes that will build your resilience, which we will examine, giving you a valuable tool to help you develop each one.

Optimism

Having the confidence that you are competent and effective will give you the strength to work well in tough times and so is the basis for your resilience. Do not think of this as a mindless 'glass half-full' kind of optimism that is blind to reality. This is about being able to see reality objectively and to match up your resources with your opportunities, to find ways to make positive change.

By keeping a clear focus on what is most important, you will be better able to spot ways to resolve issues, so start by taking stock of your goals and objectives and remind yourself what is most important. Second, inventory your resources: what knowledge, skills and experience do you have, what can your team members do individually and together, and who else can you call upon? What physical resources are available to you, too?

> as you start to break your problems down, prioritise the components against what matters most

Now, as you start to break your problems down, prioritise the components against what matters most, and allocate resources to the parts, you will start to feel in control.

🔍 brilliant tool: ABCDE

When you really feel that events are getting on top of you, apply the ABCDE approach to your situation. This is one of the most powerful tools in cognitive behavioural therapy.

Adversity   What are the events that have triggered your feelings that you are under pressure and struggling to cope?

Beliefs	Your feelings are triggered not by the external events themselves, but by the beliefs you attach to them. What are your beliefs about what has happened?
Consequences	What consequences do those beliefs have for you in limiting what you could do? How do they change your options and opportunities?
Disputation	Challenge any beliefs which frighten you or limit your options ('limiting beliefs'). Ask yourself what evidence you *really* have to support those beliefs. What alternative interpretations could you place upon the events, which would give you more power over them? For example, rather than:
	'This is another example of my bad luck …'
	try:
	'These events are out of my control, but I do have control over how I respond.'
Energise	What are some practical steps that you can take, which will give you control over your response to the events?
	'These events are out of my control, but I do have control over how I respond. I will get the team together and allocate three groups to: stabilise the situation, look for a long-term solution and communicate with our stakeholders. Since stabilisation is our top priority, that is where I will focus my attention at first.'

Gratitude

It seems odd to talk of gratitude in times of adversity but, from personal experience, this can turn around deep feelings of help-lessness and depression. Used proactively, it can help you keep a healthy perspective on events. If you do find you have slid into some level of despondency, then it is a powerful way out.

When you face tough times, set aside some time to think about what is most important to you, that you are grateful for. This will help you to put your adversities in context. Too often all that we can see in tough times are the troubles that face us. By purposefully considering everything we have to be grateful for, we recover a sense of balance.

↗) brilliant tool: gratitude journal

If you find yourself slipping into despondency, then start a gratitude journal. Get a new notebook and, every evening, make a note of one thing (or more) that you feel grateful for today. It may be a big important part of your life, like the love of your partner or having a roof over your head, or it may be a small incident during the day, like a shared joke or a compliment for something you did. You will find that, after a few weeks of this, your troubles will seem fewer and you will feel a lot more content and able to cope with more setbacks.

Here is a list of some of the things I have been grateful for in tough times.

- My team
- Past successes
- My family
- My health
- A book recommendation
- Colleagues
- A nice home
- Past experience
- Training I have had
- Techniques that make a difference
- My friendships
- An evening out
- A small victory
- A good cup of tea
- Being trusted to do the job

Flexibility

Flexibility, or adaptability, is your capacity to find new ways to deal with trouble. Keep a focus on what you want, but allow yourself to keep trying new ways to get it. Under pressure, it is usually the people who are most flexible in how they adapt to the situation that are most likely to thrive. This means looking for more and more options, when you have failed time after time to achieve what you want:

If at first you don't succeed ...

... try, try something else.

Take a look back at the SCOPE process that you read about in Chapter 11: Stop – Clarify – Options – Proceed – Evaluate. This is the basis for harnessing your flexibility in a controlled way.

---

brilliant tool: step up – step down

If you are going to continue trying more and more options until you succeed, it pays to have a process for generating creative alternatives. The 'step up – step down process' is the basis of all creative thinking.

Our normal mode of thinking is to start with what we want to achieve, and to step down by asking 'How?' and generating as many options as we can.

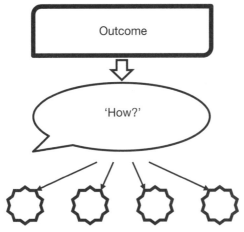

The step down process

When none of these options works, start by stepping up, by asking 'Why?' and getting at the real purpose of what you want to achieve. Then ask 'How else can I achieve this purpose?' This will give you one or more alternative outcomes that would serve your purpose. You can then step down from these and ask 'How' you can achieve this revised outcome.

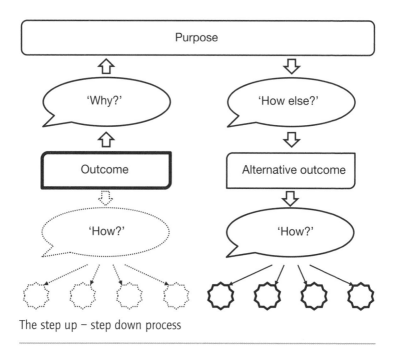

The step up – step down process

Emotional leadership

Successfully resolving the crisis or handling the problems your project faces is really just your reward for motivating and supporting your team. They will be the ones who achieve the great things. But they too need the resilience and confidence to work effectively in the tough times. So provide them with the leadership that will allow them to be optimistic of success, grateful for the resources they have together and individually, and flexible in their approaches to resolving the situation.

Perhaps the hardest thing for many leaders to do is to trust their team in the toughest of times. But this is what you must do: you must let them know clearly and without reservation that you have confidence in their abilities and that what they are doing is important and worthwhile. Give them encouragement and practical support, and also be available to support them emotionally. Listen to their frustrations and worries and address them honestly, and praise their efforts – even when the outcomes are not what you hoped for.

You can think of emotional leadership as having six levels:

1 Self-awareness, self-discipline, and taking responsibility for your behaviour and choices.

2 Expressing your emotions to create trust and respect.

3 Managing your emotional responses to achieve resilience and control.

4 Being aware of your team members' emotional states and the general mood of your team.

5 Being able to influence the emotional states of others and to guide the mood of your team.

6 Being able to support the resilience of others in your team, to enhance morale and well-being.

Political leadership

Political leadership is influencing the network of relationships within and beyond your organisation, to further the needs of your project. This requires skills in influence and persuasion, bargaining and negotiation, and networking and alliance forming. This is a big topic in itself and is the subject of a companion book, *Brilliant Influence*. Here, we'll introduce a few simple tools to help you with each of these three elements.

Influence and persuasion

You influence most persuasively when you exhibit all of the outward signs of credibility, and you back that up with genuine authority. So:

Look the part

Make a strong positive personal impact by taking care of your appearance, maintaining a good posture and smiling to show your confidence.

Establish your credibility

Make sure that people know your expertise and experience by harnessing your credentials and the support and testimonials of others.

Make a strong argument

Check your facts, use rigorous analysis and present your case in a logical and compelling manner.

Make emotional contact too

A strong argument is rarely enough. Build rapport and appeal to emotion as well as reason by using simple, concrete language and real, personal examples.

Harness the support of others

Build the support of one person or group at a time and use the support that you have to influence the people you need to persuade.

Bargaining and negotiation

Negotiation is a process, so if you follow it through its stages, then you will have the confidence to succeed.

Stage 1: Preparation

If you do not prepare, you will not succeed. Be clear about the range of acceptable outcomes and where the boundary is between an acceptable negotiated agreement and your best alternative to a negotiated agreement – your 'BATNA'. Find out what you can about the people you are negotiating with.

Stage 2: Opening

Enter the negotiation by making a strong and confident personal impact. Open things up by establishing the ground rules and who has what authority to agree a deal. If your desired outcome is a radical departure from what your counter party is expecting, state this upfront. Otherwise, encourage them to state their outcome first.

Stage 3: Bargaining

Your first bargaining position should always be 'no'. If this fails, then make concessions, with three rules:

Rule 1 – never make a concession without securing a concession in return.

Rule 2 – always make your new concession smaller than the last one.

Rule 3 – never make a concession that takes you past your BATNA.

Step 4: Closing

When you get to an end point in your bargaining, always close the negotiation by seeking formal agreement from both sides that this is the outcome.

Networking and alliance forming

Networking is one of those 'love it or hate it' activities. But it is really little more than getting to know the people around you, in a wider circle than those who are part of your day-to-day work. The more you know one another, the better placed you will each be to offer and request favours. As you get to know people, you will also get a sense of who shares interests with you and who is able and willing to support your project. If you can do minor favours for these people, they will remember this and be of help and support when your project needs it.

Staying tough

In tough times, the stress and pressure on you can take their toll on your health. So one of the most important skills for a project leader is the ability to manage your stress levels and take care of your mental and physical well-being. *Brilliant Stress Management* is a companion to this book and emphasises that stress arises when we feel that we are not in control of events, our environment, or of ourselves. So the way to manage stress is to take control.

> the way to manage stress is to take control

As a project leader, you have more control than most over your environment and the events that play out, and you read in the section on optimism at the start of this chapter how to use the ABCDE process to strengthen your sense of control here. Gratitude and flexibility will give you a strong sense of mental control, so let's focus here on maintaining your physical well-being.

There are three primary areas of control. Even in the toughest times, you must ensure that you get good fuel, good exercise and good rest.

Good fuel

Literally, you are made of what you eat and drink. In tough times, it is easy for the quality of your diet to slip and slide into rushed gobbling-down of rubbish food at the wrong times of day. Making the effort to eat good-quality food – and to take your time in eating it – is a vital investment in your health. If the bulk of your food must be fast food, then supplement it with fruit and easy-to-eat raw vegetables to give a good injection of fresh vitamins.

You do know what is good for you and what is not. Your choice of what you consume will have a huge and rapid effect on your mood and your response to stress. Why do nicotine, caffeine, excess sugar and fats and various drugs have such a massive impact on our bodies? It's because they contain powerful active chemicals. In most cases, it is this powerfully high biological activity that renders them highly toxic when used to excess.

Another important thing to note is that your brain is like a grape – or a raisin. Small shortages of water – well below the level that triggers fatigue or headaches – cause your brain to shrink and wrinkle up. This diminishes its effectiveness and makes it harder to get problems in perspective and solve them. Keep drinking fresh water to stay at your best. Keep a large glass of tap water on your desk at all times and drink when you fancy.

Good exercise

Regular exercise reduces your need for sleep and generates the hormones that activate your parasympathetic nervous system, which takes care of the maintenance and repair of your body. Under crisis conditions, regular exercise can be the first to go, and this can trigger sleep problems too. This will have a great effect on your mood and your energy levels during the day.

It is no coincidence that the busiest people take rigorous steps to protect regular exercise time. If all else fails, find a way to increase the proportion of your journey to work that you do on foot or by bike. Getting off a bus a stop or two early will not lose you much time, but the brisk walk can give you time to work things out, as well as pumping up your immune system and improving your posture.

Good rest

Make time for activities that promote effective relaxation and unwinding from the day's pressures. For some people, it may be reading, painting or watching movies; while for others it is going out, socialising or playing a sport. If you want to promote deep relaxation, why not try massage, aromatherapy or meditation?

Get yourself a sleep ritual. Do relaxing things for at least an hour before you are ready to go to sleep. Create a regular routine that tells your body it is getting towards time to turn off for the night. Avoid stimulants like caffeine and alcohol for the last few hours of the day – they have a disruptive effect on your sleep. And if your sleep is disrupted by a nagging feeling about what you need to do tomorrow, it is far better to turn the light on for a few minutes and write it down than to lie sleepless and agitated for an hour.

Brilliant behaviours

By now, you should be well able to create your own list of brilliant leadership behaviours. These are the behaviours that attract people to follow you in tough times as well as easy times. Here is my list.

⬈ brilliant list

Here is a list of some brilliant leadership behaviours.

- Enthusiasm
- Positivity
- Encouraging
- Empowering
- Open minded
- Fair
- Clear thinking
- Supportive
- Dynamic
- Flexible
- Engaging
- Collaborative

- Generous
- Courageous
- Passionate
- Compassionate
- Outcome focused
- 100% integrity

 brilliant recap

- Resilience is your ability to cope in tough times. You can boost it by taking an optimistic stance, being grateful for what is good rather than concerned about what is bad, and being flexible in your responses to situations.

- It is important to look after the emotional needs of your team in tough times.

- The three skills of political leadership are influencing, negotiating and building a network of alliances.

- Remember to take care of your physical well-being by getting good fuel, good exercise and good rest.

To lead: some closing remarks

 **brilliant** definition

Lead (liːd) 1. vb. (leading, leader, led) to guide the way by going ahead

We have examined your role as project leader from three perspectives:

1 Personal leadership: the traits, behaviours and characteristics that show you very much in control of yourself.

2 Leadership of other people: what it takes to create a desire to follow your lead.

3 Leadership of project activities: directing what goes on in your project and responding to the circumstances that arise.

The next bend

What we have not considered is one final aspect of leadership – your ability to stay ahead of events. For many years, I have been drawing a simple symbol on a board at training events and seminars.

This symbol represents 'the next bend'. A vital role for any leader is to be able to see around the next bend in the road and

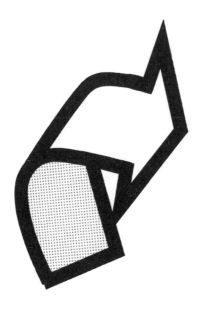

The next bend

anticipate what is coming. However, this is not about fortune-telling or prophecy. It is simply about reading the road.

But you can only do that if you give yourself the time to notice and reflect on what is going on. This means *making* the time. At least once a week, step out of your normal environment with nothing but a notebook and pen. Sit and relax, go for a walk, or get a coffee and a cake – it doesn't matter what you do as long as you give yourself time to think. Ask yourself questions like:

- What is happening? What are the events, patterns, trends that I need to be more aware of?
- What is this telling me? What are the things I have missed, and the implications of what I already know?
- What is around the next bend? What are the things that are going to happen, which I have been unaware of, at a conscious level?
- What do we need to do? What are the actions I need to

initiate now, or soon, to stay ahead and prepare for what is coming up? How can I positively influence the future?

If you are unable to make the time to look ahead, events will come to dominate your agenda and you will fall behind. This is not leading; it is following.

The OODA loop

Colonel John '40-second' Boyd was a US Air Force fighter pilot in the Korean war of the 1950s, who went on to write an aerial-attack study that became the fighter-tactics manual for air forces all over the world. He never lost his standing bet that he could get behind any fighter that was on his tail, within 40 seconds.

His analysis of air superiority and why the US fighters were so successful in Korea (78 US F-86 fighters shot down, compared with 792 Russian and North Korean MiG-15s) led him to articulate his idea of the 'decision cycle' or 'OODA loop'. In an environment of imperfect knowledge and rapid change, good situational awareness and manoeuvrability were the deciding factors.

A project is also a rapidly changing environment where your knowledge will be incomplete and you may be unable to observe everything with precision. So here too, good situational awareness (taking time to look around the next bend) and manoeuvrability (or flexibility) are critical. Boyd's OODA loop is a cycle of:

Observing the situation

Orienting yourself to reality, or comparing what you learned with your existing understanding to create a better model of what is happening

Deciding what to do

Acting with determination.

Then cycling back to observe the outcome of your action, orienting yourself to the new information and making your next decision.

Boyd asserted that if you can go around the OODA loop rapidly enough, you will gain control of any situation.

Brilliant project leader

Give yourself time to notice what is happening and think about what it means. Make your decisions and act decisively. Support and inspire your team. Behave with absolute integrity. Good luck.

Glossary of common project management terms

Business case An analysis of the benefits and costs of making a change to the way things are done.

Change control A process for managing requests for change in an auditable way, to ensure that only appropriate changes to the project are undertaken once it has received approval. Also ensures that where changes are authorised, appropriate additional resources are allocated.

Contingency An amount of time, budget or functionality incorporated in the plan beyond the project team's best estimate of what is needed, to allow for the adverse impact of risks.

Contingency plan A plan developed to mitigate the outcome of a risk, once the risk has materialised.

Controls Controls set out how you propose to stick to your plan in the face of the challenges of the real world, and what you will do when reality forces your project to deviate from plan.

Cost breakdown structure (CBS) Hierarchical presentation of project costs, usually derived from the *WBS*.

Crashing the deadlines Making compromises to advance work ahead of schedule, or to catch up a significant delay.

Critical path   The sequence of tasks in the project that define the shortest time the project can take. Tasks on the critical path, if delayed, will cause a delay in project completion. Critical path analysis (CPA) is the process of finding and evaluating the Critical path.

Deliverable   Also called *product* or output, the thing that the project produces (physical thing or event).

Dependency   Some tasks can get done at any time and are independent of other activities. Others are linked to events like the start or completion of other tasks. These linkages are called dependencies.

Gantt chart   A tool developed by Henry Gantt that helps a project manager to plan, communicate and manage a project. Shows project activities as horizontal bars, with a length that represents the duration of the task, and places them against a fixed timeline.

Goal   States the over arching purpose of the project – what you seek to achieve. Also known as 'aim'.

Impact   The change of outcome resulting from a threat or opportunity.

Likelihood   A measure of the probability of a risk occurring – often based on an interpretation of how often similar risks have occurred in comparable past circumstances. Therefore sometimes referred to as frequency.

Linear   Chart showing responsibilities for each

Milestone   A significant event in the life of the project. Alternatively, a marker of progress (either large or small).

Mitigation   Any action designed to reduce the likelihood or impact of a risk.

Network chart   Planning tool that shows the logical sequence of project activities.

Objectives   These set out the measures of success that you will apply to achieving your *goal* – typically in terms of time, cost (or budget or resources) and quality standards.

Organisational breakdown structure (OBS)   Hierarchical presentation of project team members, according to the work they are assigned to. Derived from the *work breakdown structure*.

Plans   Plans set out how you intend to deliver your project. They address the three project elements: tasks, time and resources, and describe what needs to be done, how it will be done, when, by whom, with what assets and materials, and how it will be paid for.

PRINCE2™   *PRojects IN Controlled Environments*. The UK government's methodology for project management. It is maintained by the Office for Government Commerce (OGC), the government agency that is responsible (among other things) for project management in the UK public sector.

Product   Also called *deliverable* or output, the thing that the project produces (physical thing or event).

Product breakdown structure (PBS)   This sets out all of the *products* (or *deliverables*) of your project in a structured way – hence articulates the scope of your project.

Programme   A portfolio of projects and initiatives managed together – sharing something critical like joint objectives or a common resource pool.

Programme evaluation and review technique (PERT)   An estimating technique that starts with a *network chart* and combines optimistic, best estimate and pessimistic estimates to produce an overall estimate of the most likely duration and standard deviation (spread of likely durations) for a project activity.

Project An endeavour that stands out of the ordinary set of activities. It has clear start and end points and produces a defined outcome. It is a coordinated set of activities.

Project board Governing body of a project – ultimately responsible for the oversight and decision making. Sometimes called the project steering group.

Project brief Also called terms of reference or outline PID (project initiation document), sets out the definition of what the anticipated project is (and is not).

Project life cycle Sequence of phases of the project from beginning to end.

Project management The process of managing a project. Deploys tools, processes and attitudes that deal with the complexity and uncertainty inherent in a project.

Project sponsor Also referred to as project executive, senior responsible owner (SRO) or project director. Represents the needs of the organisation to the project and the needs of the project to the organisation. Acts as 'manager' to the project manager. Part of the project governance process, the sponsor will either contribute to, or be wholly responsible for, oversight and decision making.

Responsibility chart team member, against a list of tasks, or work streams.

Risk Project risk is uncertainty that can affect outcomes. Risk can introduce a positive (opportunity) or negative (threat) change.

Risk appetite The level of exposure to risk that you are prepared to tolerate.

Risk register   Formal document and management tool that records all risks identified by the project team, along with the team's assessment of the risks, plans to manage the risks, and progress against the plans.

Scope   All that the project must do and create. It can be expressed in terms of activities, articulated by the *WBS* or in terms of deliverables, articulated by the *PBS*.

Scope creep   The tendency for people to sneak extra work and outputs into the project's list of responsibilities. Can cause a project to fail under the burden of additional work without the corresponding resources.

SRO   Senior responsible owner – a *PRINCE2^{TM}* term for the project sponsor.

Stakeholder   Anyone with an interest in your project – whether affected by its outcome or process, or with an ability to affect its outcome or process.

TCQ triangle   The time–cost–quality triangle, also known as the iron triangle, triangle of balance or the triple constraint.

Team   A team is a small number of people who collaborate to achieve a shared goal.

Virtual team   A team that does not work together physically all of the time.

Work breakdown structure (WBS)   Formal tool that breaks the project (the work) down into a structure – allowing a firm inventory of tasks, in a logical hierarchy.

Work package   A defined chunk of work, usually contained within a single work stream.

Work stream   A subset of the work breakdown structure that is allocated to a single manager: the work stream leader.

Appendix 1

Mike's rules

Scattered through *Brilliant Project Leader* are some of the many 'rules' I have observed in over 20 years of leading projects, training project managers and speaking on the topics of projects and change. Here are the rules articulated in this book, gathered into one handy list.

Mike's first rule of teams
You get the team you deserve.

Mike's first rule of communication
Honesty is not the best policy ...
... it is the only policy.

Mike's three rules of change
Rule 1: Resistance is inevitable.
Rule 2: Always respect your resisters.
Rule 3: Some people will welcome the change. Make them your allies.

Mike's three rules of negotiation
Rule 1: Never make a concession without securing a concession in return.
Rule 2: Always make your new concession smaller than the last one.

Rule 3: Never make a concession that takes you past your BATNA.

Mike's first rule of meetings

Start on time.

Appendix 2

Learn more

Also by Mike Clayton

All of Mike's books will help you to become a brilliant project leader.

Brilliant Influence

… will give you advice, tips and solid psychology that will help you influence stakeholders and get your team members to meet their commitments. It also gives you more details about how to negotiate, build networks, exchange favours and present your vision powerfully. Particularly supplements Chapter 12.

Brilliant Time Management

… will help you to manage your personal time, so that you can stay better in control of your agenda. It also has specific guidance and ideas about how to make your meetings more effective and delegate tasks to colleagues.

Brilliant Stress Management

… will help you to stay tough in tough times, by giving you resources to control your response to stressful situations. Particularly supplements Chapter 12.

Handling Resistance Pocketbook

... will help you to deal with resistance to your project and the changes it is designed to bring about. It has fuller details of the onion model and also applies it to other situations. You will find many techniques and tips for handling resistance here. Particularly supplements Chapter 10.

Management Models Pocketbook

... describes in more detail some of the models used in *Brilliant Project Leader*, including the OODA loop, Tannenbaum & Schmidt, Tuckman and the drama triangle. Other valuable models for project leaders include Vroom's expectancy theory and McClelland's model of motivational needs.

Risk Happens! Managing risk and avoiding failure in business projects

... is all about project risk management. Like *Brilliant Project Leader*, it is targeted on new and less experienced project leaders, but focuses entirely on risk management. It also contains a lot of material that will be valuable to more experienced practitioners.

Shift Happens!

Mike's blog on change, projects and risk is called *Shift Happens!* and is at www.mikeclayton.wordpress.com.

Other books that you will find valuable

Brilliant Project Management, Stephen Barker and Rob Cole (Prentice Hall, 2009)

Effective Leadership, John Adair (Pan, 2009)
Particularly supplements Chapters 2, 3 and 4

Team Roles at Work, R. Meredith Belbin (Butterworth-Heinemann, 2010)
Particularly supplements Chapter 2

Coaching for Performance, John Whitmore (Nicholas Brealey, 2009)
Particularly supplements Chapter 2

Leadership and the One Minute Manager, Ken Blanchard, Patricia Zigarmi and Drea Zigarmi (Harper, 2011)
Particularly supplements Chapter 3

The Wisdom of Teams, Jon R. Katzenbach and Douglas K. Smith (McGraw-Hill Professional, 2005)
Particularly supplements Chapter 4

The Wisdom of Crowds, James Surowiecki (Abacus, 2005)
Particularly supplements Chapter 7

TA Today, Iain Stewart and Vann Joines (Lifespace Publishing, 1987)
Particularly supplements Chapter 10

More on leading projects and related topics at
www.brilliant projectleader.co.uk

Index